Crooks,
Bankers,
&
Politicians

...a primer on the American Economy

By Jake Street

Other books by Jake Street

The Texas Water War

Political Fiddlefaddle

DEDICATION

J. Collier Adams, Jr.,
an attorney who describes himself as
"just a West Texas county lawyer and landowner"
roams the wilds of Cochran County, near Lubbock, Texas.
But Jay or James,
as called by his friends,
much like another Adams of American History,
is a serious thinker;
especially, when it comes to land law,
private property ownership rights, and
equal treatment under the law
as guaranteed
in our American Constitution.

And all
who value freedom
should dedicate something
to James Adams.

CONTENTS (pages)

ACKNOWLEDGMENTS

Before acknowledgment, there must be recognition of why it's needed: why should something need acknowledgment?

So, any attempt at looking at the economy must ask, "What is the job of an elected official, say, a United States Senator or a Governor – or even a city council member?"

Is their job to accomplish acts that will improve the nation, the state, or the city in which they serve?

Think about it.

Sure, everyone wants to have something to point to and say, *I did this* or even, *I helped do that . . .*

But *not* doing something is often more important than doing something.

So, what is their job?

Is it a *fiduciary role* (relating to or based on a trust)?

Just as the relationships of bankers, attorneys, CPAs, and most professionals with their clients or customers are based on trust, so are citizens' dependence on government built on trust – to the value of their money to protection from enemies within and without - to being let alone by a limited government that acknowledges responsible freedom in the pursuit of happiness.

Today, a lot of people are unhappy with government because they have lost their trust in government to do those things –

Government has grown because most of those we elect promote the interest of government, *not ours*. Most elected officials have *failed* in their fiduciary roles.

They are – or become – servants to the government, not to the individual citizens they are Constitutionally-mandated to serve and protect; and swear an Oath to do so.

It is hard to serve two masters, *so it is written.*

Consider Congress: Are those we elect trustees for the citizens of their states or for Congress? Much as many may claim differently, they cannot be trustees for both.

Just as an attorney cannot represent both sides in a legal dispute or a real estate agent cannot represent both sides in a real estate deal, a member of Congress makes his or her *choice* to represent either the citizens or the government.

We, the editorial we, understand that government employees have a fiduciary trust to their employer, the branch of government that hired them. Their duty is to act in the best interest of that governmental unit. This is not necessarily in the interest of their friends or what *they* may think is best – or the citizens. As trustees, they are the administrators of the government's business, not the citizens – just as a City Attorney represents the city and not the citizens.

But a member of Congress is the trustee of those who elected him or her; not for the government, nor for their state. As trustee, they are to serve and protect the interest of all citizens, not just a few acting as lobbyists or a group representing some special interest. And sometimes, they are *required* to protect citizens from the actions of government.

Or even protect against unconstitutional acts of the administrative and judicial branches.

For instance, if a governmental department or agency fails to do its job or has performed it illegally, a Congressional member who fails to hold that agency or department (or the employees) accountable has failed as the citizen's trustee – just as surely as those carrying out the wrong action(s) have failed as trustees to the government.

Doing wrong is not included in their respective jobs.

Protecting citizens from government encroaching on individual liberty, the rights of private property ownership, equal economic opportunity and, in general, assuring equal treatment under the law for all citizens, are part of the requirement for being a trustee of the citizens.

Under the Constitution, a Congressional trustee's job is to stand between a government that wants more power, more control, more government, and the citizen "yearning to be free."

A fiduciary trust is not an easy burden.

To do it wisely is not easy.

Anyway, America is now buzzing about ISIS, Muslim terrorists, falling family incomes, the rich-and-poor divide, abortionists, gun control, infrastructure (including oil and gas pipelines), giving nuclear weapons to Iran, Putin, claims of climate change, and a bunch of other stuff that costs semi-good money.

When it comes to our trustees, most often, it seems we're getting the cart before the horse's rear.

Especially, when we don't know where we're going or how we're going to get there.

So, the acknowledgment must be that it is no wonder we're losing trust in our trustees . . .

1 Stupid is as Stupid does....

*Once upon a time...*America had the greatest economic system the world has ever known.

Then we started electing socialists to office who wanted to make their friends and families rich.

Most of these politicians, and those who purchase politicians, think the only way to have a centralized government and make money is to keep poor people poor.

In 1955, Walmart – our nation's largest employer – did not exist. Neither did GPS, MP3 Players Ebay, Google, Microsoft, Apple, Dell, Amazon, I-pads, Smartphones, Websites, or ObamaCare. Franchising was barely a gleam in a promoter's eye. Oil was selling for around $5 a barrel and, if you had an oil well, you could only pump oil five to 12-days a month. And in China, people were starving.

Economically, you would think that nowadays things should be great –

Yeah, you would *think* it . . .

But, then, the Washington crowd started changing things. And today, if it would help them to stay in office, they would steal a dead fly from a blind spider.

Even in 1975, "equity" financing was illegal, viewed as a "mafia" operation.

And now, we think it is okey-dokey for one of the major political parties to elect a CEO of an equity or venture capital firm to be President of the United States. And if that doesn't stimulate a few brain cells, consider that, if the polls are right, 25%-or more – representing 80-million of 320-million Americans – would support a self-proclaimed socialist for President.

What is really, really, painfully pitiful is that more, even a majority of voters, may support Honest Harpy Hillary, a *lying* socialist who knows she is lying and those supporting her know she is lying, and they simply do not care.

But that ain't the bottom of the rotten barrel: The Washington Republican crowd, if you put them in a bag with Democrats – and shook it real good – would be like a sack of cats: You can't tell any difference in the cats in the bag.

All you would know about a bagful of the Washington crowd is that they stand for anything we will fall for –

Isn't progress wonderful?

It is part of the *dummying down of America.*

Socialists hold that people, in general, don't know what is best for them, and that they need someone who can take care of them. That is, someone who is just naturally more intelligent and better educated and more responsible and, likely, better looking.

Of course, this system only works if one very superior person makes all the decisions –

– but I don't want the job . . .

And, yes, there is a reason why I don't want the job: Failed harvests, oak wilt, locusts, fire ants, droughts, floods, lawyers, chambers of commerce, the West Nile

Mosquito, and other such natural calamities make even the most ardent socialist quickly engage in an over-consumption of some bottled and bonded Tennessee Tea, which leads to weird habits and shocking behavior.

Plus, you know how government and unions work; you can't get experience without experience.

So, voters have turned running the country over to a handful of *less* superior people.

But they are really doing a great job of *ruining* the country.

Surely, what has and is happening is more ruining than running?

History teaches that it is the educated and responsible in high places who try to kill each other. They just use the young and physically fit to do it. Their favorite way is the use of a "limited police action" to get what they want (*war* is such an ugly word). And that way, they don't have to win to demonstrate what powerful leaders they are (and *winning* is so unfair)!

A few bodies are a small price to pay to get what they want.

A few hundred thousand bodies are a small price to pay to bring their brand of enlightenment to the world. Besides, *those young people* were messing up the environment and contributing to climate change.

And it eases the socialists' fear of the scarcity that ol' Hardin observed in his *"Tragedy of the Commons"*, in which his paucity of observation boils down to "there is nothing we can do to improve our lives, so the herd needs thinning."

Hardin, evidently educated beyond his level of comprehension, is a great phil'os'afer to socialists everywhere.

But socialists, as other socialists claim, have *a good heart.*

Socialists know that those heartless Conservatives are just *unreasonable* people who don't want to send youngsters to fight a war in some corner of the world to *protect* the human rights of the oppressed to take the property of others and, who, if they must fight a war, want to win it at all costs to the enemy. (*Those damned insensitive, uncaring clods!*)

When what they believe in doesn't work, socialists know that it is because there is just so much bad luck in the world ... especially, if you believe in the social and economic equality of all people based on *"from each according to his ability, to each according to his need."*

But the control of all means of production espoused in a *"from each ... to each"* philosophy means that slavery is the only way to achieve it.

All production starts with an individual.

And that is the reason for this small primer on what should be the day-to-day economy in the real world – and not the overblown stuff of wild theories.

This is about the results from what you do and what your neighbors and friends do; about how and why and what happens. And a couple of other little things that relate to your personal economic well-being.

This is economics made simple, based on one fundamental fact: Every economic system only starts because of and by the energy of the individual.

It may be yours.

So read on . . .

2 Economic Opportunity (and Collateral)

In the mid-1980s, those good ol' bozos we elected as our representatives and senators (and still do), to serve our interest, sold us out to the big money boys.

They allowed the nation's banks – along with stock brokerage and insurance and mortgage firms – to become financial institutions, allowing each to do what the others did, and adding all of them to the welfare rolls.

Bankers, who are supposedly the experts in lending and establishing interest rates, thought it was highly unfair that they were accountable for bad calls the incompetent among them made. So, they paid Congress to authorize a few regulations creating the adjustable interest rate.

This did several things, none of them good.

The first thing it did, it removed accountability from the judgment and the decisions of bankers.

Previously, to be successful, bankers had to research and study and made decisions on what the economy and the interest rates might do. But removing accountability from financial institutions meant that it had to go someplace.

Accountability has to be some place.

So naturally, in the scheme of political things, accountability ended up on the taxpayers and lower level consumers. The adjustable interest rate policies forced taxpayers to socialize irresponsible decisions and actions of a lender.

A lender, who had used bad judgment on the rate of interest charged on a loan, could "adjust" the rate amount. This eliminated long-term loans at a fixed rate of interest: an economic necessity among small businesses owners and the nation's job creators.

Short-term loans rapidly replaced long-term loans, allowing the new financial institutions to adjust terms of the loan as well as well as the interest rates. Lenders could renew the loan or revise the terms or extend a new loan – or refuse to loan.

Do *not think* about the wonders that the adjustable interest rate did for the nation's housing markets.

And taxpayers were now accountable for the success of the new financial institutions, as they were *"too big to fail."*

Lending practices quickly turned to extending loans with payment calculated on a long-term payout, but with a large "balloon payment" of the remaining amount owed at the end of the short-term loan. This kept all of the payments reasonable, except for the final one.

With a wink and a smile, borrowers were assured that "a new loan" would be available when needed, at the end to cover the "balloon payment". But when that time came, some bankers claimed they were "unable" to rework or renew a new loan for the remaining balance, as things were beyond their control. But –

Friends of some bankers suddenly were able to pick up a promising, profitable business on the cheap when the owner was unable to make a required balloon payment tacked on at the end of one of the new short-term loans.

Mergers and buyouts suddenly were popular.

Compounding the negative effects of know-nothing politicians, or those the bankers were buying, the removal of accountability for decisions on what lending policies and interest rates might do over a five or ten year period or to the national economy in the future, basically did three things:

It eliminated long periods of stability in the nation's market places. Business and economic planners were unable to say with any confidence or accuracy what the economy would likely do. The up-and-down surges in interest rates created a related movement in stock and commodity markets.

Speculation – rather than investment and savings – became the new purpose of stocks and stock markets. Big money speculators started making huge bets on when the markets would go up and down. Wide market swings meant more profit. The only losers were the nation's small stock investors, 401-k retirement type funds, and a few businesses that were not too big to fail.

It changed the rules on lending. The new rules removed value from assets for lending purposes, replacing the acquiring of assets with an existing cash flow for loans. This essentially declared assets were no longer a form of savings and, henceforth, any established and current assets would be collateral.

The new regulations removed banking restrictions against a previous list of recognized unethical negative and *criminal* practices.

For years, people with money that they didn't immediately need or did not have a use for, could invest it in a bank that would pay them a fee for doing so.

The bank acted as an intermediary, loaning the money, in turn, to those that had an idea that seemed likely and one that was likely to pay back the money. For this service, the intermediary would charge a fee for use of the money. (A fee that was always slightly larger than the fee the bank paid to the depositor.)

These loans were for the purpose of acquiring assets, something that had value, whether for acquiring land, a building, tools, equipment, fixtures or inventory.

All these things are a form of savings, just as is the purchase of a home.

But the new regulations were for cash-flow loans, not assets. Banks could only lend on money flowing thru a cash register. So assets were suddenly collateral. The bankers loaned on the established cash flow, which a planned new startup does not have – unless is an outlet for an existing tasteless franchise or chain or big box store.

For years, if you have enough assets – land, building, equipment, cash, etc. – banks would loan you part of the appraised fair-market value, but not on the full estimated value. But now, banks do not loan on assets. If you have an existing cash flow, a bank may make you a loan, but they'll treat your assets as collateral, not assets, and they will take a "vested interest" in those things.

A "vested interest" is a form of ownership. For instance, you participate in a company's retirement program. You have a "vested interest" in that part of the fund that holds your account. You are the owner of that part, but you do not own all the funds in the retirement program.

In short, a vested interest is a form of ownership and the lender is staking a claim of ownership in all the listed collateral.

Under asset-based lending, where the money loaned created assets, a form of savings, there was an equal economic opportunity to improve one's life and the lives of their families.

Without a way to acquire assets, economic opportunity is restricted to only those who have money or who have friends with money.

This does not meet any Constitutional requirement of "equal treatment under the law."

In 1970, Congress aimed the RICO Act at mafia type endeavors: An example being when, in lending money, the lender demanded part of the business ownership (equity) in exchange. The Act stated that *extortion* was against the law. But with the changes in the mid-1980s lending regulations, equity funds and venture capital funds were the new way of doing business.

Congress legalized extortion.

Now, equity and venture firms take the intellectual property, the idea, as well as the assets of others in exchange for loans they require repaid, usually at a high rate of interest.

When the only "choice" you've got is to do it their way that is not a choice.

Today, in the land of the free, the only menu is limited economic opportunity, served with extortion on top.

This translates into the fact that too many Americans are forced to perform on terms demanded by their economic masters; something the 13th Amendment to the U. S. Constitution absolutely forbids . . .

3 Crooks, bankers & Politicians
-- *a primer on the economy*

Like millions of Americans, I'm tired, fed-up, a wit's end, and disgusted with know-nothing politicians and government economists talking about "creating jobs".

The "jobs" they are yakking about are punching time-cards in a dead-end slot for some worldwide monopoly or conglomerate – or as an under-employed, part-time captive to a fast food outlet, a franchised chain, in one of the big box stores or, most likely, as another government parasite in a new or expanding government program.

That is not "job creation" - it is economic slavery, which is a dammed poor way to build an economy.

Most jobs are not industrial or governmental jobs.

There are millions of bakers and candlestick makers, artists and computer programmers, plumbers and electricians, pot throwers, glass blowers, car salesmen, marine operators, surveyors and engineers, attorneys, construction workers and carpet layers, jewelry makers, website developers, real estate and insurance agents, designers, doctors and homecare specialists, inventors and taxi and uber drivers, painters, lawn mowers, tinkers, etc.

The American economy is composed of every kind of self-employed and small business owners – from apple-pickers to zoo designers, and more – who outnumber by millions the number of monopoly and conglomerate employees.

It is a world of independent individuals and small business owners with five or six-or less employees.

But these are jobs exceed all the jobs of Big Business and Big Government combined. And none are the *idea of a job* as defined by our nation's Crooks, Bankers, and Politicians.

But they are the kind of jobs that have disappeared and are disappearing because of the change to State Capitalism, the welfare-partnership between Big Business and Big Government.

America – prior to Lyndon Johnson's guarantee to the Federal Reserve Board that the government would guarantee all loans to the foreign countries his administration would recommend – had the greatest economic system the world has ever known.

That system – the Private Enterprise System – created economic opportunities for those willing to work and who were responsible for their debts and honest enough to pay their bills. It created for all Americans the world's most powerful economic engine, the highest standard of living, and moved millions out of poverty.

But LBJ, much like progressives today, had no doubt that government is the answer to everything. And when a reluctant Congress, faced with billions needed for the Vietnam War, started cutting back on foreign aid, Johnson believed he had discovered a way to bring countries who were not our friends under his influence. It was his "come, let us reason together" all over again, which had worked so well during his years in the House and Senate. His ego (even larger than he was) assured him it would also work with foreign leaders, even those who hated us . . .

Countries who knew they would never pay back the money, gladly took it nevertheless. Even those who did intend to pay back the loans were facing interest rates up to 15-16 percent.

The big banks making the loans also knew that most countries would not (or could not) pay back the money. But using a "high risk" factor as an excuse, they charged an interest rate well above those charged here at home. And with payment of principal and interest guaranteed by the government, the banks didn't care, as there were no risks to them.

Next, when the nation's oil companies created the first false oil shortage, came Jimmy Carter's executive creation of the Department of Energy (DOE). Under this new DOE, oil and gas prices spiraled crazily upward.

In Texas, where the Railroad Commission for years had held the pumping of oil by wells to only five to twelve days a month, with the increases in prices, the oil well pumps were working 24-hours a day, seven days a week.

But not just oil prices were increasing.

Interest rates were also climbing.

Banks were demanding rates that compared with those guaranteed by the government on the billions of dollars in outstanding foreign loans.

Those needing money had to borrow at these higher interest rates.

With the increase in interest rates, banks, savings and loans, mortgage firms, insurance companies, and other financial institutions were shoveling money out to every over-priced, risky scheme and semi-crooked (and a lot of not so semi-crooked) deal that came their way.

And the nation's businesses, large and small, needing new loans to meet this increasing inflationary costs of doing business, had assets that were already mortgaged to the hilt with loan ratios exceeding over 100% of market value in many instances.

By the early1980s, their deposits mostly loaned out to foreign countries and no repayment coming in, bankers begin yowling like tomcats in a moonlight night for the government to make good on its guarantee.

And the crooks, bankers and politicians got together with a bunch of actually stupid people and sold out the Private Enterprise System, exchanging it for State Capitalism, the partnership of Big Business and Big Government.

The Crooks got the system; the bankers got their financial shenanigans guaranteed; and the politicians and the government secured the control of it all. (Additional background on background is found in the chapter, *Quicksilver Funds.*)

American voters allowed it to happen. Voters swallowed the lies that something from nothing is possible; that government can return more than they take by some magic multiplication factor. So now, when we look in the mirror, the stupidity we see should be frightening.

Currently, all across America, big banks establish outlets in small communities and use their local deposits for big cash flow loans to big businesses that are located outside the branch office communities.

Economically, we have lost our way.

For America to get back on track, for all Americans to have a chance at the brass ring, Congress must:

(1) Immediately authorize the creation of private community or neighborhood banks where loans are restricted to below $500,000, and that 40% of all deposits must be used to make asset-based loans for new business and other economic start-ups within the community. Or

(2) Establish a provision in current banking regulations that 40% of the deposits of the community where a bank is located must be used for asset-based loans, below a $500,000 maximum limit, for new economic start-ups within that community.

Before dismissing the recommendation, think economics: Today, all we have are Big Financial Institutions loaning money on deposit to only Big Businesses. And many of these conglomerates or monopolies use the funds borrowed from Americans to build outlets and strengthen markets in foreign countries.

Consider these facts:

The economic reality is that, for years, we – America - created a racket in trade and finance with little risk and great rewards for the Big Money Boys, with a guarantee that the taxpayers would reimburse any of their losses.

We let the nation's big bankers, who know better, tell us that our assets – things that create wealth and riches – are worthless; and that only a "cash-flow" system of financing was worthwhile. We bought this nonsense.

So bankers started swapping a lot of shoddy paper and washing illegal drug money (for the big fees that could be generated for the fortunate few and finding ways to make hordes of dirty money clean). This, the bankers said, was worthwhile.

They lied.

Banks started as a fiduciary trust: To act as a go-between for those who have money they need to put to work and those who have a good idea that seems likely to succeed, but need money to bring the idea to market.

Banks came into being to bridge these two needs, and they made money by charging a fee for the confidential services. They made money available in small increments (for the provider's safety) to *create assets* for thousands of small businesses. It was an asset-based value-system. And it *created the greatest economic system the world has ever known.*

But we let the nation's big banks stop banking. We let them start selling stocks and insurance and promoting all kinds of worthless paper scams. Our financial institutions stopped banking and started pie-in-the-sky schemes for bigger fees. In exchange for money flowing into their political pockets, our politicians let lenders force the change from assets to cash flows on local community banks.

And small, practical, good ideas based on asset-development, that seemed likely to succeed, began to die from lack of funding.

And as they died we stopped making good things and offering all kinds of service, and economic choice died.

When this change to financial socialism started, many of us warned it can only destroy the value of *all* assets, including the dollar.

But our politicians told us that the world had changed, and we had to change. So, Americans scaled back on doing the constructive things and constructive work by letting those in charge eliminate small asset-based loans.

Soon, all we had were a few international firms doing business in a world market.

Beginning 1990s, we started killing the nation's independent small businesses.

Too many small communities are now just a few "name franchises" and a few of the same-name big box stores scattered around the outskirts of once very vital downtown areas. And selection and choice are dying, too.

This is the cold reality of today's new economic world.

During the 1980s, Congress removed restrictions on the type and kind and size of loans a bank could make, replacing them with regulations that gave unfair advantages to big business. This killed off the nation's "mom and pop" type of small businesses, which had been creating over 70% of all the nation's jobs.

New regulations in the late 1980's required the nation's banks to use a business's existing cash-flow (instead of assets) for lending purposes. This was a policy creating economic opportunities for established endeavors, but killed new venture startups (as new businesses don't have cash-flows until after the doors open).

As part of the new regulations, Congress allowed formation of "venture capital firms" that soon also became known as "equity firms". Regardless of title, both demand part of the ownership of any endeavor they finance.

But for decades, there were restrictions against lenders demanding part ownership of an endeavor in exchange for the financing. In the eyes of the law, this was a practice used by "the mafia" or organized crime. And in 1970, Congress passed the RICO (Racketeer Influenced and Corrupt Organizations) Act, which was to combat organized crime in the United States. It established prosecution and penalties for such actions as BRIBERY, money laundering, illegal gambling, drug trafficking, sexual slavery, and a whole host of other unsavory practices.

So within a decade, what Americans once viewed as a criminal activity performed by crooks (bribery) became approved "capitalism" by our nation's government and the big new financial institutions and economic geniuses working for both Big Business and Big Government.

In the real world, several economists, who value words and their meanings, saw it as devolving the meaning of "criminal" to "equity firm".

Organized crime activity became the foundation of America's new "Capitalism": A way of demanding that the total amount of a loan be repaid, with a high rate of interest, in addition to demanding part of the ownership interest.

Less than 20-years after removal of restrictions against such activity, one of the owners of an "equity" fund was a candidate for President of the United States.

In one decade, this change created opportunities for *opportunists* with money to lend – by allowing them to act as parasites on the ideas and talents of others. But at the same time, it *denied* economic opportunities to those with assets; basically removing value from the ownership of assets, as the owners could no longer borrow money on those assets.

This change from restrictions to regulations traded our nation's Private Enterprise System for State Capitalism - the partnership between Big Business and Big Government, America's new form of socialism.

While Americans may not know why, they generally know there are too many recent years of falling family incomes and a widening gap between the haves and the have-nots, of a government reporting job increases that are part-time jobs.

We can see the vacant buildings in too many small towns (where small businesses once created jobs and their assets served as family savings), and they understand that average Americans are facing less choice and no equal economic opportunity.

In general, Americans realize that no candidate for a national political office is offering a solid economic platform that they will or can emotionally endorse and support. They have heard the talk for over a quarter of a century, but have seen no positive results. And they (we) are desperately searching for a way out of the economic mess we're in . . .

Assets – the land, buildings, equipment, inventories, fixtures, furniture – are all a form of savings.

A cash-flow is only made possible by using an asset

– even if it is drug trafficking or sex trafficking or slavery.

But asset-based lending require personal character, integrity and honesty, which are not required for cash-flow only loans.

This little primer on what should be the American economy may never see the light of day. But it should; it's needed; it is worthwhile. And as far as being affordable, America cannot afford not to abide by Constitutional constructs for *equal treatment under the law* and the equal economic opportunity (which cash-flow policies do not provide).

4 State Capitalism

Up until the last 30-or so years, America was a land where *individuals* were free to use personal choice for improving their life. There was the freedom of an equal opportunity to acquire assets and private property ownership rights were Constitutional guarantees.

Under these guarantees, a private enterprise financial system evolved: Individuals could pool their surplus money with a known and trusted middle-man, who would lend it to other individuals who needed money for an idea that would likely pay for itself and who were likely to pay back the money. And the middle-man charged a small fee for his services.

This created a banking system where those with money (beyond their day-to-day needs or who had no idea for its use) could earn money by allowing the neighborhood banker to make their money available to those with an idea, but who needed money to purchase the assets by which to pay it back, with interest.

It was a banking system where local banks made small, asset-based loans for business and community development within their local area. Up until the mid-1970's, it was hard to find a bank that would make a loan above $500,000. Above this amount, loans were available from insurance companies, commercial mortgage firms, and short-form SEC offerings (selling shares to raise money).

This financial system created wealth and riches; the world's highest standard of living for millions and millions of Americans. It made America the greatest economic force in the world . . .

But in the late 1970's, politicians in both parties started changing the rules.

Using *government guarantees* for purchases, a few national big banks gobbled up the nation's smaller banks. By the 1980's, new endeavors to create small businesses could no longer find *loans based on assets*, only on cash-flows (which new businesses do not have); and the *minimum cash-flow loan* amount wanted for such purposes had climbed to a jaw-dropping *$3 million and over.*

And average Americans were no longer able to participate *equally* in this new system of State Capitalism.

Equal treatment under the law – supposedly guaranteed by our Constitution – disappeared.

Today, our financial system is economic nonsense: All we have are a *few* big "financial institutions" making *only* multi-million and multi-billion dollar *cash-flow loans* (and earning big fees), huge multi-billion dollar "hedge funds" manipulating stock markets (for big fees to guarantee *their profits*), and "equity-funds" that provide money in exchange for "part of the deal."

Today, only *the deal* between the insiders is important.

Accumulation of private assets, a form of savings, and the creation of opportunities for local economic development, have no role in today's excuse for an economy.

Now, all we have for economic enterprise is world trade and a handful of a few expanding franchised chain stores, fast food outlets, and big box stores – with all the transactions guaranteed by our rapidly-expanding centralized government.

Politicians created laws that killed community banks and independent small businesses and, in their place, created purveyors of paper: Stocks and bonds, commodity and insurance brokers, equity purchasers, quicksilver firm investors, promoters of derivatives and other strange instruments all under a "financial institution" umbrella – *everything but a bank!* And now, we are in a system of *economic plunder* – a socialistic partnership between big business and big government – that has nothing to do with capitalism or private enterprise.

America became the world's power under a private enterprise system of *asset based lending,* where local deposits were re-invested in local communities by *local* community banks. The key words being "local" and "banks" – not the huge, largely flawed, "financial institutions" of today; created by politicians *as vehicles for big financial deals for a few key insiders* who, in turn, would finance their campaigns.

The private enterprise system created diverse, strong communities.

And jobs.

And opportunities.

The professional liars and talking heads tell us that our entrepreneurial "capitalistic" spirit will get us out of this mess.

But creating more government, bigger deals, more subsidies, more tax loopholes, adding more debt, borrowing more money, printing more money, declaring a "small business" is one with an annual $3 million net cash flow, eliminating economic opportunities and telling lie after lie, is a recipe for creating economic and social disaster.

Isn't this what has happened?

So how can we expect that what got us into this mess we're in can get us out?

Everyone but politicians and the brain-damaged know that the end results of acquisitions, mergers, buyouts, takeovers, and cash flow lending policies: Reduced employment, elimination of competition, less quality in brands, fewer services offered, and reduced economic opportunities, and a lowering of family incomes.

But as we slide ever deeper into the pit of State Capitalism, even conservative and libertarian-leaning politicians claim that "correcting the tax structure" or "eliminating regulations" will *solve* our economic problems.

Well, no, they won't...

And the economic idiots in both major parties, and those who directly benefit from such actions, keep calling for "enhanced revenues" and "stimulus money" to *fix* the problems that such actions helped create. And know-nothing "moderates" gripe about *political stalemate*.

El-Yucko.

Only political stalemates have saved us from even more digestion of our forced-fed economic socialism.

All we have for an economy anymore are a few large conglomerates and monopolies producing enormous amounts of inflated money, which they see as "profits", and which they share generously with both major political parties, the U. S. Congress, some highly-placed law enforcement officials, and financial buddies.

Economic opportunity has been reduced to *giving someone* a substantial share in *your* startup endeavor for peanuts – or giving them a big fat fee – usually upfront.

These are paths to economic collapse.

Confused talking heads are giving us hokum about today's "capitalistic" system needing "to be set free" to restructure the economy and, in Congress, their political counterparts are giving us more hokum about how government needs "to step up to the plate and bring fairness and balance" to "our economy".

They all weep together, while spouting crap about "creating jobs"!

All of it, the same *political crap* that messed up the greatest economic system the world has ever known.

How can jobs be created when what we're doing is killing economic opportunities?

America no longer offers economic choice - a concept (unique in the world) where individuals had the freedom to improve their life by the acquisition of personal assets - in a land where private property ownership rights are honored and individuals have an equal freedom of opportunity to acquire assets, all of which are constitutional guarantees, *and law punishes predatory practices.*

The world's seekers of freedom saw this system of private enterprise as America: In their minds, *"The Private Enterprise System" was America.*

Every dictator, socialist, communist, bleeding heart, every destroyer of mankind, saw America – this Idea of America – as everything they feared and everything they hated.

As here in America, the emotionally damage, the weak-minded, the power hungry, all the little birds-of-a-mental-feather, listened to the siren call of the world's deranged and began to destroy the very things that made America great.

We, who should have known better, joined the chorus of the mentally sick and voted into office some of the most mentally deranged among us.

But whom do we vote for...?

Not one single national candidate, nor all of them bundled together in their $1200 suits, provided by lobbyists, have the slightest idea of how to "create jobs' - or the courage to restore the Private Enterprise System.

We have lost America - thanks to our votes for know-nothing politicians.

State Capitalism is a controlled blend of private and public endeavors.

It is a system where the state is intervening in the market to protect and advance the interests of Big Business.

It is in sharp contrast with the ideals of both a free market and a laissez-faire private enterprise system.

5 a model for failure...

China is the model of State Capitalism.

A Chinese endeavor, whether it is building high-rise offices, apartments, manufacturing computers, or cutting and sewing the latest in women's and men's fashions, is in partnership with the government. It is a blend of private enterprise and socialism (where the state is a partner in the actual enterprise or is in control of most every decision). The endeavor can only succeed with the blessings of the government.

In 2009, we said that, *"Like Japan's economy of the 1960-1970s, much of China's supposed boom is illusory — and will likely come crashing down."*

We said it because State Capitalism – a watered-down form of Communism or Socialism – will not work over the long-term.

Economic systems that carry obvious contradictions cannot survive over extended time.

And yet, our economic and governmental leaders are busy creating more State Capitalism here at home.

How bone-deep stupid are we?

An economic system of State Capitalism cannot satisfy the basic needs of the citizens it holds under its top-heavy embrace. But because it is, however, a social welfare partnership between Big Business and

Big Government, its weaknesses are seldom revealed until the final collapse.

The Chinese economy today parallels that of Japan in the 1970s and 80s — immense accomplishments co-existing with immense failures.

In some ways, China's stability today is more precarious than was Japan's before its fall. China's poor are poorer than were the Japanese poor, and they are much more numerous: About one billion in a country of 1.3 billion. Even worse, the gap – as has happened in all State Capitalistic systems – between rich and poor increases.

And this is the emerging pattern in the United States of America.

State Capitalism is nothing more or nothing less than lawless capitalism, a system of a few getting rich quickly by awarding themselves and their friends the bribes of those in charge of the government. It is nothing more or nothing less than government giving or selling access to the economy in exchange for "political contributions" or job placement after office, with the unspoken knowledge that whatever the government subsidizes the government controls (sooner or later).

This is a system of corruption. Today, the public acceptance of corruption is pervasive — big fees and even bigger favors for a select few. And they are now enriching themselves enormously.

This corruption deprives the poorer among us of their homes, livelihoods, health, and restricts the freedom of their lives.

Under State Capitalism, enforcement of existing laws are corrupted, not only in regulatory standards for financial dealings but extending to health and safety and public services and everything that affects our personal lives.

Executives, paying themselves high salaries (for leading their financial institutions into failure), are rewarded by billions of "stimulus" money from a government that collects the funds from millions of Americans working for basic wages.

Financial institutions that only made big loans based on big fees from big companies stand in line for trillions of "free government money" before, during and after the stimulus bailouts.

And evidently, many Americans applaud this corruption that is inherent in our growing system of State Capitalism.

Social security *reforms* enabled our government to collect $2.6 trillion (accumulated in a combination of taxes collected and earned interest from workers) from the Social Security Trust Fund and spent it (waste it) on whatever.

These *reforms* left the fund filled with IOUs from the U.S. Treasury. In any objective judgment, it was theft, a criminal activity.

Even a progressive's twisted mind should recognize that it was a corruption of the very meaning of the words "trust fund."

Both major political parties are responsible.

But do we hold the politicians who voted for these "reforms" responsible for the theft? Nope, we continue to re-elect them to office until they can retire safely out of Washington, and live happily on their large and inflation-protected pensions for public service.

Isn't our failure to demand accountability a corruption in our personal sense of responsibility and accountability?

Meanwhile, it is becoming more and more obvious that our economic system of State Capitalism – modeled after that of China, and other current world systems – has created our economic downward plunge, and the reason why economic choice and economic freedom are dying.

We have a few getting rich and a lot more growing poorer...faster.

And we are all mindlessly shouting "U-S-A" at the top of our voices with all the power of our lungs, while embracing stupidity with both arms.

China is buying us with our own money. And when China's system of State Capitalism goes, which it will, our system of State Capitalism will follow.

Instead of divorcing ourselves from State Capitalism and renewing America in our once-great system of Private Enterprise, we are embracing failure.

But government is never benevolent. Politics, by its very nature, it depends upon Karl Marx's adage, "The greater good. . ."

And government survives by an economic policy of "Might Makes Right."

State capitalism rose in Japan, following the end of World War II.

In a desperate effort to rebuild their nation and economy, the Japanese government and banks staked out key areas of mutual concern. They developed policies to assure success in their approved economic attempts to rebuild. The major and most far-reaching policy being that, in exchange for money loaned to finance such an attempt, government and banking officials would occupy management and Board of Directors decision making positions in Japanese business endeavors.

Beginning in the decade of the 60's, with a booming world economy, this early model of aggressive state capitalism grew Japan into the world's foremost economic competitor.

Seeing Japan's success, business and industry leaders screamed to political capitals about what they saw as "unfair" competitive practices.

Many countries, already leaning toward socialism, created governmental partnerships with supposedly private firms to push for economic gains. And Politicians, eager for power or money, created some favored status for select economic segments within their country's borders.

The Japanese policies of putting all economic eggs in a basket of government partnerships created a long-term fault-line or weakness within their own economy. As they became the major economic force on the world economic stage, they ignored their own internal economy. And the Japanese economic bubble burst in the late 80s.

The yen lost it power, and the Japanese market lost most of its gains. Today, Japan still has not recovered from its failed experiment with economic socialism.

Ignoring the Japanese experience, other countries continued to set policies for expanding into state capitalism.

China's entry into world markets coincided with a remarkable growth of policies in world capitals creating governmental partnerships with receptive sectors in private endeavors.

Urged on by such "humanitarian" countries as the United States, China's leadership blended their form of communism into economic partnerships that could compete in world markets.

Today, there is not a single Chinese industry competing internationally that is not in partnership with the Chinese government. But China is not alone.

America is right there with China.

Today, there is not a major difference in the economic systems of China and America. Both are engaged in State Capitalism, a partnership between Big Business and Big Government.

And both countries are now seeing confusion and unrest in their economic systems.

There is not a major American financial institution that is not in some form of partnership with our government (loans and deposits are guaranteed by government and the right to a profit guaranteed by the Federal Reserve Bank).

In 2009, America's nationalization of the nation's

financial institutions was a result of those banking partnerships. The big financial institutions were no longer subject to failure.

Our national leaders said so, arguing that they were *"too big to fail..."*

And Congress passed laws in agreement, making it the law of the land.

There is not a major U.S. industry that does business in a foreign nation without some form of guarantee by the American government.

There is not a major oil company not in partnership with some government in the world today.

There is not a major U.S. endeavor doing business here at home without some special privilege or advantage granted by the government. For instance, taxpayers are funding research and development programs for the big oil and big drug companies, thermal energy, electric and wind power generation, and for the protection of our *international* firms.

These are supposedly private sector enterprises in partnership with government.

The misguided (or ignorant) talking heads in America, including conservative Rush Limbough, call it "Capitalism" — leaving out the silent word, "State".

But there is not a spit's worth of difference *in principle* between what America is economically doing and what China's government is doing.

American enterprise was to be private.

For years, the American economic system was a "Free Enterprise" system. Then, after government had dropped so many special advantages on some, and restrictions on others, it became a "Private Enterprise" system.

It wasn't free to do business anymore.

The basic excuse for governmental intervention in the free enterprise system was the social argument that *"in the real world property rights and contracts, which are the basic requirements of a functioning free market system, require coercion or physical force in order to be upheld, a true free market by this definition is impossible."*

The weak-minded failed to recognize the falseness within the statement, which fails to acknowledge the rule of law in a free society (and assumes or substitutes the law of man).

Under private enterprise, Constitutional law, *not the government,* guaranteed equal economic opportunity.

Law set the rules within the system. But special interests, insiders, the power-hungry, and the plunders, corrupted the law, perverted it, giving themselves (man), the power to coerce and use physical force (police action) to get what they wanted.

With its nose in the door, soon all of the government-ass was in the room. And now, like the Chinese, Americans are living in a system of State Capitalism.

We, America, got here because we did not pay attention to the business of politicians.

Too many of us believe the business of politicians is the creating and passing of laws for the common good. This is not so. The business of politicians is getting money or power – or power and money. And it is the same in Austin, Tallahassee, Pierre, Sacramento, Little Rock, Albany, or in the capital in your home state.

And in Washington, D.C., or in Japan, Russia or England, or in some remote village in "Hijackastan", the greed for money and power is the same.

In every government department you'll find some affable but stupid or greedy bozo cluttering up and covering up and creating special privileges for someone.

In politics, we're told there's no black or white, only shades of grey, and that there is no good or evil; just degrees of right or wrong.

And in both parties, the party is the most important thing. . .

Why should we expect more?

The goal of each party is to put a "spin" on truth; on facts. The only objective is to make the respective party look good and expand their power and sources of income.

It is a political party's promise of things it cannot deliver that encourages socialism.

Society, unfortunately, is a concept generated by cultural, social, ethnic and economic groups who bring the failures of "the old country" with them or who become the victims of "educationalists" at some university teaching history from their government paid position.

The primary concern of the socialist, they tell us, is the welfare of the people, especially the welfare of the poor, the old, the disadvantaged and the minorities. The answer to the problems of these, they claim, is government.

They ignore the fact that a private enterprise system, operating under a limited government that assured all citizens an equal economic opportunity, created the greatest wealth for the greatest number of people the world has ever known. And it created more wealth more quickly, while providing the greatest liberty for a "pursuit of happiness".

Limited government did it, not a form of socialism.

The conservatives wants government to do things their way, based on some perceived Biblical instruction, whether its abortion or liquor by the drink: Forgetting that any government with the right to tell you what you cannot do also *has the right to tell you what you must do!*

The libertarian trades away individual rights for the unrestricted rights of monopolies and conglomerates.

These are organizations that care little for the rights of individual workers and, unchecked, end up, like government, seeking control of everything within the boundaries of their own little worlds.

Worst of all, are the disgusting promoters of "ethnicity"— History and a little common sense show that ethnicity offers no cultural benefits or advantages, except for those promoting their own personal brand of ethnicity as a way to make money or gain power. They are demagogues, using lies to capture the stupidity of those looking for someone to blame for the conditions they find themselves in...

Sooner or later, State Capitalism will fail. Socialistic systems always have, and eventually always will.

For over three decades, we (the editorial *we*) have warned of the dangers of State Capitalism. We watched it expand, while warning that it carried within it the seeds of its own destruction.

But too many who can see the results, are so emotionally handicapped or mentally deranged they *want more government in order to control what the government has created.* They want government taking money from some and giving it to others. This illogical desire, if carried to its illogical conclusion, would only create more government, more socialism.

Today, the results are a nation under siege by its own government.

Banks, Financial firms, car manufacturers, oil companies, healthcare, and business endeavors of all kinds are coming under the control of some faceless government bureaucrat or power-brokering Czar.

And there are the stupid – no matter how smart or intelligent they may be in other matters – who believe that the answer is more government.

According to the U.S. Treasury Department, our debt in the middle of 2015 was at 93% of our Gross National Product (GNP), and will be at 102% in five years.

At a debt equal to 90% of GNP, nations lose 1% of their GNP per year.

And we have idiot's in national leadership positions, in both parties telling us that we can spend our way to prosperity by adding more debt.

And we keep re-electing them to office.

We elect and re-elect and re-elect them, saying that we do it because "we're democrats" or "we're republicans" or "libertarians".

But that is only partially true.

The real reason we do it is because we are bigger idiots than the ones we elect and re-elect to office. They, the ones we elect, are smart enough, at least, to grow rich and powerful on our stupidity.

We like to sip and/or smoke, sniff or inject a little something while sitting around some social get-together and proudly sizzle about our New Knowledge, about how much smarter we are today than those of a short generation or two ago.

Everybody that is anybody is on Facebook. We all have a Twitter account, along with a new car with all the latest gizmos, a Big Hair House with thousands of square feet under roof, all the latest computerized appliances, and every available "app" loaded on our latest "smart" phone (an "app" being advertising we pay for in order to get advertising by sites selling the "app").

And we have a lot of other things that have little lights that come on and go off.

We're New Knowledge cool.

But let the central air and heating unit go out and life is miserable until the technician in the dirty shirt shows up. Let the Microwave fail to pop the popcorn or heat the prepackaged meal and we're running to the nearest tasteless fast-food outlet (one of a chain and all selling the latest "fresh" food). And when that new car won't answer the bell and whistle...there's the call to the ole boy with a little grease under his fingernails.

When the holders and proud processors of this New Knowledge run headlong into a new, high-tech or old low-tech problem, they call the low-ranked folks with old knowledge to bail their arrogant asses out of the hot water or unsolvable fix they're in –

No one is asking what will happen when the crops stop growing, when the chickens stop laying eggs; the bacon runs out, and the animals of the fields are not sacrificed for steaks and pot roasts? No one is asking, "How will my New Knowledge save me from starving?"

New Knowledge of how to cut a deal on some other guy's idea, how to buy a politician, how to get the inside track on the latest legal vegetable to smoke, or even how to build a better app, can't plant and harvest the crops or cut up the meat or keep the wheels turning or change a fuse.

The old knowledge was a structure of honesty and thrift and being responsible, knowing you would be accountable for your actions.

But New Knowledge is a rush to get what you want while believing that anything goes.

It's knowing how to work in partnership with government, and how to use other people's money to make you rich. It is believing that the best people are those making the most money and getting the biggest bonuses and retiring early with millions of dollars annually, while ignoring the fact that the socialism you're practicing is playing favorites for a few and millions more are losing out, and sometimes it's hard to look in the mirror.

Socialism is not New Knowledge – no matter what we call it or how much we dress it up in bright and colorful words. Underneath the paint and polish, she is still the same old slut that kills hope and opportunity.

For roughly 200-years, the Presidency of the United States was a respected office and generally the President was held in high esteem. But since the days of Clinton, it has been a glorified business – or, at least, a mighty fine racket.

And so is being a *Congressperson.*

Voters have allowed progressives to turn America

into a different country.

The problem is that the progressives have never truly said what country they want us to be.

The basic bureaucratic imperatives are to escape responsibility, dodge problems and gather power to themselves...they make up rules, regulations and laws as they go along.

And these are the reasons why everything run by government is botched or messed up. It doesn't matter whether it is Katrina or Sandy or Homeland Security or Healthcare or the Department of Education or the IRS or the CIA. It just does not matter.

Whatever government gets involved in, it eventually takes over and fouls up. So, all you Exxon-Mobil, GE, Monsanto, and Wal-Mart types, beware!

What the socialist, the conservative, the libertarian, the ethnic leader, all of us, forget is that no coffee tastes as good as it smells.

All newly-weds learn that there is a difference between anticipation and realization.

Only voters forget.

But how could they forget, when America's future is a nation of economic slaves and social servants to a centralized government in charge of everything?

6 Results of State Capitalism

Encircling the globe is a financial crisis that is the doing of the United States.

We created it, and we are paying a steep price for doing so.

We created this financial mess by exchanging our Private Enterprise System for State Capitalism, the partnership between Big Business and Big Government.

America – at the urging of internal home-grown socialists – imported a watered-down version of old world socialism, buffed and shined it, painted it up, and by offering it as something different, we enhanced and endorsed it, and exported this "new system" to the eagerly waiting vultures of world government.

In doing so, we signified our approval and endorsement of centralized government to a world struggling for economic freedom. (As personal freedom cannot exist without economic freedom, we gave America's blessings to economic slavery.)

We did so because we had lost our economic identity: economic freedoms assured in Constitutional constructs of equal economic opportunity.

We did it out of weakness, because we listened to those who destroyed our banking system, exchanging banks for a few large "financial institutions" pedaling insurance policies, stocks, bonds, commodities, and a world of worthless paper with strange names and very little to no value.

In exchange for high fees for "loan origination" and "brokering", this allowed these new financial institutions to shovel out gobs and gobs of dollars to a few big companies and conglomerates; corporations that used the deposits of an unknown number of small investors to build and operate overseas.

This change in our economic system also allowed an increasing number of progressive politicians to shovel out trillions in a currency they were rapidly devaluing to an increasing number of big government programs that could, we have found out, waste the dollars as fast as their friends in the legislative side of things could hand them out.

Under an umbrella of "progressivism", a watered down regurgitation of socialism and other failed theories of governmental centralization, we accepted economic policies foreign to our private economic system.

Today, the world's economic mess, and ours, is the result of the change from our American Private Enterprise system to State Capitalism.

Know-nothing talking heads call it "capitalism" – a transitory nomenclature – but there is no recognizable difference between today's "capitalism" and "State Capitalism" (socialism). Even the etymology shows there is no difference in meaning between the two terms.

The partnership between Big Business and Big Government is now our economic system – as it is in China, Russia, Japan, and most every country of the

World. The only minor exceptions are those countries ruled by absolute dictatorships, such as Cuba, Iran, Syria, North Korea, etc., where the totally centralized systems subjugate such partnerships to total control.

The Big Banks adopted new ways of financing that provided the funding for bigger, but fewer, economic endeavors. Politicians passed laws that made the creating of "partnership" efforts easier, and opened the door to more and bigger partnerships.

"Big is Better" became our national motto. By the early-1990s, State Capitalism was in full swing here at home, and the Private Enterprise system was a thing of the past. No longer were we a "bright shining city on a hill", but just another dim bulb in a world of dim bulbs.

Communist China, facing economic disaster and growing population unrest, broke from Marx's vision for communism, and allowed government insiders to form private banks and corporations. The government retained large blocks of shares in these new ventures, keeping varying amounts for their own ownership, and encouraged the Chinese people to own shares in them.

Instead of meeting this new economic challenge, America's progressives endorsed it.

What we are now enduring is not one of the usual "business cycles" that our economic leaders bring about every few years. It is the result of State Capitalism's failure to "manage the economy".

The results of Japan's failed venture into State Capitalism are obvious. Over the last two decades, the Japanese stock market plunged down, losing most of its value; inflation of the Yen almost went out of control; and the national debt is at an all time high. This nation, once feared as a competitor in world markets, is no longer an economic threat.

Does this history begin to sound familiar?

This time, America's "downturn" is likely to be here for a much longer term. It may stretch into distant years unless we make basic changes in what we have done to our economic system. If we continue to try (repeatedly) failed *economic stimulus* programs or seek to re-invent with new names the same policies that forced State Capitalism on us, real pain is coming our way, and the pain will linger for years.

We measure our cyclical recessions of the economy by *The Great Depression.* In many ways, our current economic situation has dangers exceeding those of that period.

Too many of our "economic experts" keep telling us that our economy will come back bigger and better than ever "just as soon as government can make a few changes"; as soon as *the government* can "create jobs" and "invest in our future".

But our "experts" don't have the least idea about how to create jobs.

How can you create jobs when you don't know how – or what a job really is?

Americans are told that our economy, like the ocean tides, is subject to rise and fall and that it will always come roaring back. We have heard the false promises until we're sick of them: Business is "picking up", industry is now starting to re-hire, retail and wholesale sales are increasing, and opportunity is just around the corner – as soon as government can tinker with a few more fixes and corrections.

Or they will if you elect me...

Today, like the non-thinking morons we are, Americans are waiting for "government" to bring us back – forgetting that government got us here.

We have come to accept the idea that government is the economic gravity that controls the economic tides. When it comes to government, we will believe most anything, even though it is not true.

For years, our political and economic leaders told Americans (and are still telling us) a lot of things that were and are not true, not factual. And based on these lies, we now have an economy that will not – cannot – "be a tide lifting all boats".

When we changed to State Capitalism, we shoved economic choice and equal economic opportunity into a dark cellar and locked the door.

Under State Capitalism, we went wild for special favors for special people who could and would generate big fees. We stopped asset-based lending and replaced it with speculative cash-flow financing for mergers, buyouts and takeovers - everything and anything even though it reduces the number of jobs, eliminates competition, and restricts economic opportunities.

We closed manufacturing plants for good, sold all the equipment, and moved the jobs overseas. We stopped making a lot of things. In doing so, we eliminated millions of jobs; jobs that will not be coming back, anytime soon.

We allowed our banks to stop being banks and become huge financial institutions promoting everything and selling everything – including economic opportunity.

We created a system where only the ultra-rich, and those who had the means to pay high fees for an entry into a private world of high finance, could play. We allowed financial institutions and stock promoters to sell us junk bonds, over-priced shares, derivatives, worthless mortgages and to do things with our money that should have placed them in jail for long terms.

The nation's con-artists point to a climbing stock market where, every month, our government drops in around $80,000,000 of the taxpayer's money to prop-up stocks and save the overpriced and falling stocks manipulated by Hedge funds.

Like with most government programs, all we are doing is subsidizing a perception.

We let banks stop making small, asset-based business loans for inventories, equipment, fixtures, buildings and operating capital.

We watched passively as small businesses died (the backbone, the foundation, of our previous economic systems). We accepted a cash-flow only loan policy that reduced choice to big box stores, a franchised name, tasteless fast-food outlets, and a few monopolies or conglomerates.

We let the banks adopt the adjustable interest rate to protect them from responsibility and accountability for making bad decisions. And this gave us the *adjustable rate mortgage,* which has done so much *for* the Big Fee Boys and done so much *to* the American taxpayer.

We told homemakers and others they could no longer work at home to earn or supplement family incomes by or on piecemeal work; a policy that forced working mothers to pay for a baby-setter, in order to find a job outside the home. And the same policy eliminated numerous income-earning opportunities for the handicapped and others.

We did this because such work activity limited government on ways of collecting income taxes, to carry out demands of unions favoring wages over production, and because the large firm's desire to eliminate any possible competition.

We set minimum wage requirements that drove inflation and created job losses, in exchange for too-powerful union leaders offering political endorsements. As wages were set at inflationary highs, it drove many chances at part-time employment and most entry-level jobs out of the marketplace.

All these things that killed economic opportunities are just a small part of the economic stupidity we have endorsed under State Capitalism.

How can we have an economic rebound without a way to sustain a recovery? As long as we are playing in a world economic system of State Capitalism, what or who will lead our economic comeback?

If State Capitalism got us into this mess, how can it get us out?

If it cannot, and it cannot, where is the opportunity for recovery, or increasing prosperity and new economic growth for America? Certainly, subsidizing a few big businesses and even larger conglomerates and monopolies is not the answer.

How can we depend upon the falling economies of a Greece, Italy, Ireland, or the stagnant economies of a Great Britain or Germany? Do we place our hopes and our future in the worrisome State Capitalism of China and India, which are showing slackening demand and many changing internal processes and pressures?

Yet, we have a blind hope that our politicians, who created the State Capitalism mess we're in, are going to get us out of it?

Get real.

These are the politicians with the same philosophy. Politicians who killed the private enterprise system, destroyed it to meet the idiotic failed theories of socialism and its off-spring, State Capitalism.

More of the same thinking that got us in this mess is going to get us out?

Isn't that like claiming that in order to preserve freedom it must be up to government to control it?

The reality is that State Capitalism can only offer an increasing loss of personal and economic freedom, a lingering recession, the danger of a looming on-going deep depression, with raging inflation in our food and energy requirements – and a near-future nation under total centralized control.

Do we – does America – have the leadership necessary to process and adapt to this reality? Are we prepared to return to our economic roots? If not, we better prepare for a terrible economic future.

The basic fact that we should consider is that our nation's progressives see government as the solver of all problems.

And that fact does not bode well for us as free individuals.

7 public-private partnerships
(Cronyism-at-Work)

A Public-Private Partnership is where government joins with a private endeavor to achieve a common goal, whether the goal is worthwhile or not. *As examples*:

(1) A Private Trash Company enters into an agreement with the Local City to pick up Local City's garbage because Local City does not want to operate dump ground anymore. The local Citizen continues to pay the trash bill to the Local City rather than to the Private Trash Company. Local City cuts off utilities to Citizen until the bill is paid.

A Private Store does not have an agreement – "a partnership" – with Local City. Citizen does not pay bill to Private Store. Private Store cannot have the Local City to cut off utilities until Citizen pays the store bill. Therefore, it is obvious that government does not treat the Private Store and the Private Trash Company equally, as required under Constitutional law.

(2) Private Developer and Local City "partner-up" on development of retail and residential property. The Local City provides taxpayers funds as start-

up "seed money" and gives years of property tax relief. Under government ordinances, Local City forces citizens to pay part of the development costs, as it subsidizes (gives relief of) the Private Developer's property taxes.

Another Private Developer wants to start a project, but does not have a "partnership" with the Local City. This Private Developer's request for start-up "seed money" or tax relief is refused by City. And again, it is obvious that the government does not treat both parties equally, as required under Constitutional law.

Some government lovers will not need harp lessons where they're going.

We can look ahead all we want, but under cronyism our future is in our rear-view mirror. History shows that private-public partnerships create unequal playing fields and the same rules – the same opportunities – do not apply equally.

Witness America's new socialism: State Capitalism, the partnership between Big Business and Big Government: "cronyism" is killing off small businesses and is responsible for falling family incomes. It creates a widening divide between haves and have-nots. It is generating unrest in stock and commodity markets; and it will not protect our borders.

What it is doing to America's economy is a crime. But Big Government protects its' Partner, an eager and willing co-conspirator. Government officials accept bribes as campaign contributions and refuses to enforce Constitutional equal opportunity and equal treatment mandates.

Non-essential economic private-public partnerships do more harm than good. History teaches they can even "lose" billions of dollars in unknown pockets, (think Corzine and Madoff), and lead to $600 screwdrivers and $1500 hammers.

What do the progressive/regressives that make up the United States Congress, the 100 senators and 435 representatives, the total 535 elected members, have in common, besides their far-left ideology?

They all created (a) Bernard Madoff and his company of lies, and (b) they made it possible for Madoff, and others, to milk the system – legally and illegally.

Madoff, the one-time head of Nasdaq, who brokered one of the biggest Ponzi schemes in Wall Street history, spread a liberal share of his ill-gotten billions to help further the aims of his favorite candidates and their campaigns. And he pumped a large chunk into the Democratic Senatorial Campaign Committee, a political action committee guided by ex-Senate Majority Leader Harry Reid and Senate Minority Leader Chuck Schumer of New York, Bob Menendez of New Jersey and Amy Klobuchar of Minnesota.

And one recipient of Madoff's largess, Senator John Corzine (D-NJ) later was boss of a hedge fund where over $1 billion of the investors' money disappeared. When questioned by some of his former Senate members about what happened to the money, Corzine said, "I don't know."

How in hell can you lose a billion dollars and not know *something*?

Corzine lost over a billion dollars and he doesn't know where the money went? And the poor confused liberals of New Jersey elected and re-elected this man as their U. S. Senator?

Equal treatment (equal protection) under the law is the search for justice.

Equal treatment is what voters should demand that government strive for . . .

Too often, when the government enters into a

"partnership" with a private entity, something goes wrong. Citizens seldom receive what was promised.

The prediction, that is, the promises about how it is or will be good for the economy or the nations, never seems to materialize.

One would think all that much fertilizer would grow something –

But private-public partnerships will eventually limit development.

How can they create growth?

When you start picking and choosing which individuals will or will not benefit from tax dollars, you are sowing the seeds of strife, discord and conflict.

That is how to kill an economy, not grow it.

Joining Caesar is not the same as "rendering unto Caesar" –

Any action creating special treatment for a select few is another step on the road to socialism!

Most of us may not know all the arguments of right and wrong but, nonetheless the values are rooted somewhere within us. Generally, most of us do not have a problem in recognizing the difference between right and wrong.

It may come from a rule, perhaps, demanded by our parents when we were children with a discipline enforced for breaking it. A fairy tale with a moral we read in school or even a series of challenges in high school or college that required a discovery in thought. And even more painfully, an extended time and effort we spent thinking about who we are, why we're here, and where are we going in our life?

What we gain from this totality of tears and laughter about the things that make us who we are and what we are, is what we take with us wherever we go, whenever we go where we go. It is the wisdom we gain in the pain of night that determines our knowledge of right and wrong that makes us who we are.

And we should never let others take the knowledge

of right and wrong from us – especially, by lies or wrong examples.

Regardless of what anyone may say, each of us should always seek our own individual judgment, about what is wrong and what is right, based on what worked and what has failed in the past.

Generally, an administrative bureau interprets laws that legislators create and pass on to them, and they develop interpretations – theories and procedures – until the law takes on a different shape – usually one the administrators want. And the shape it eventually takes in their interpretation is one that extends their power and influence, and benefits them personally.

And the Intent and the intentions of the law are lost.

But an "interpretation" is not always the law.

Lawyers argue over interpretations of laws and administrative actions. That is why we have courts: to enforce rules of the game (the does and don'ts), define interpretations, and establish control over how the search is conducted for truth (and justice). These are the reasons why we need attorneys.

A claim made before the court requires a much higher standard than a claim outside the courtroom.

Outside, attorneys can say most anything they want, claim any opinion they want. And there likely is an award for doing so, since they're taught how to parse a word or two, and are paid for doing so.

But as history shows, especially the last half-century, it is too bad that we cannot trust the judgment of those elected or appointed to public office; we simply cannot trust them to do the right thing.

Voters know there is an incompetency in government actions, but they – somehow – must enjoy the loss of public trust in government, as they keep electing politicians who push more programs that lead to more incompetency.

Highly contentious government recommendations

and contemplated actions should never be en-acted rapidly. On any issue likely to generate discord, there should always be a generous time-period for open and thoughtful analysis, so that a determination, based on common agreement by a recognizable majority of citizens can likely be found.

If a definite majority of citizens cannot find agreement, just don't do it.

Like driving a semi in heavy traffic, it is always better to be safe than sorry.

Those promoting government for all things have, in their twisted thinking believe that the process takes precedent over the results.

Consider that, somehow, some now find fully and completely acceptable to allow government to subsidize wind energy facilities. Plus, allow them to asks for and receive property tax abatement for the 10-year life of their equipment from local areas where the "wind farms" are located. But this creates a private-public partnership that allows wind facilities to freeload on the local school district and county taxes.

There are those in the economic development agencies who have interpreted this or, at least part of it, as being okay (probably the same ones who created loopholes in the IRS tax code).

But as reports accumulated over the years show, most of the large firms benefitting from tax relief were in violation of Tax Abatement Act mandates. They failed to comply with investment and job creation mandates governing tax relief.

The point here being that not one politician knows how to fix the economy. Not one –

The "economy" these nincompoops keep screaming about consists in their thinking of only manufacturing and stock brokerage "jobs" that come in partnership with Big Business and Big Government – State Capitalism, the new socialism.

To be fair, note that they also keep preaching about the need for "doing away with regulations" – except those that eliminate competition and make their friends and campaign donors richer.

Oh, sure, their masters, the lobbyists, want them preaching about the need for "doing away with regulations" – except those regulations that eliminate competition and/or help make their own operations more profitable.

Today, we have one self-proclaimed (and several non-self designated) socialists offering themselves as Presidential candidates; each running around moaning some version of how 1% have everything and 99% have nothing. They demand that government take 90% from the 1% and give it to the 99% (except the part the government will keep for telling the 99% whom they must vote for and how they are to live their lives...)

But what they (and those who vote for them, don't understand is that around 55-years of that fuzzy thinking is what got us in our present mess?

If you think, you wonder *why* mentally-deranged progressive/regressive/socialists think the very same thing that created the mess can get us out?

According to the U. S. Department of Labor, today there are approximately 142-million non-farm jobs in America. Manufacturing creates just under 18-million jobs, and the federal government employs around 22-million. So, together, manufacturing and government only create around 40-million jobs – with most of them being government positions. (And there around 100-million people who are unemployed; the result of government policies at work for the last half-century or so.)

But the *know-nothing yahoos promoting government* are talking about manufacturing jobs...time-card punching jobs...when the economy depends upon more than just "jobs" in manufacturing and financial institutions.

And how can they talk about "regulations" when their "laws" have created our present State Capitalism (a new name for socialism in America)?

The laws – regulations – that politicians have passed killed community banks' ability to make asset-based loans, which created small business startups – and the greatest job creating system the world has ever known. According to the promoters of government in charge of all things, as we have seen, it is the responsibility of government to oversee the creation of all jobs. But jobs created by government require taxes to pay the salaries of those holding the government jobs.

Where is there a real economic gain in that process?

The majority of jobs come from the self-employed and the small business segments. Jobs are artists, designers, plumbers, electricians; and in auto repair and service, clothing shops, shoe-stores, surveyors, computer sales and service, real estate, attorneys, authors, clerks, machine operators, landscaping efforts, the building trades, and thousands-more in non-timecard punching trades and professions, and millions and millions of small business jobs.

Politicians selfishly seeking more money and more power do not want independent jobs or small business jobs: It is far easier to control the 5,000 monopolies and conglomerates on the stock exchanges than 320-million-or more Americans.

Starting back in the mid-1980's, politicians purchased by the nation's larger banks, brokerage and insurance firms, exchanged the historical asset-based lending policies for cash-flow loans only. This created big financial institutions making risky loans to big firms that had an existing cash-flow.

This was also the beginning of State Capitalism and the downfall of the American economy.

This experiment into State Capitalism partnerships wiped out hundreds of thousands of small businesses in local communities, eliminated competition, and reduced choice and economic opportunities.

This socialistic approach to controlling the means of production allowed the cronyism that has created a nation of haves (billionaires boasting of "buying politicians") and have-nots (100-million unemployed and more under-employed).

This new American socialism ruined healthcare, education, economic opportunity; and allowed the mentally-deranged to appoint mentally-deranged Supreme Court candidates who were approved by a mentally-deranged majority in Congress.

And the Supreme Court became a national forum for Justices with personal agendas, who are destroying Constitutional mandates.

As an example, consider the whole unfortunate healthcare insurance fiasco: The same falsely inflated prices for humans now even affect veterinary costs.

Since so many people are beginning to buy pet insurance, the vets now feel they can afford to raise the prices to as much as what the insurance company will pay. This, of course, sucks for those who don't have insurance, so more people get pet insurance, which raises the prices even higher...ad infinitum...the cycle begins.

The insurance companies simply do not care: The more clients, the higher the premium, the higher the premium price, the more profit to the insurance company.

But who is at fault that you have to purchase insurance to protect yourself and your family?

In 1965, when Progressive Senator Ted Kennedy authored the Medicare Bill, a private hospital room had an average cost of $25 per day. Today, even the progressive-socialists refuse to acknowledge the result of government's intrusion into healthcare; they deny that government's intrusion is responsible for the high cost of healthcare.

Okay.

But if it isn't government intrusion, it's voter stupidity.

Consider today's dental costs: Pre-Insurance, until Medicare, prices were generally affordable for dental work. People could just pay cash. Dentists charged people by a set fee schedule, usually $2 to $5 to pull a tooth, $5 to $7.50 for a filling. But if the patient didn't have that much money and desperately needed a tooth removed or fixed and the dentist was aware that they were of a good hard-working family unable to make ends meet on a meager income, he would charge some price he thought they could afford to pay.

To some extent, this was healthcare in general.

There were farmer families who would pay in produce, carpenters who would pay in services, so the dentist or doctor sometimes had a repaired garage full of fresh cucumbers, melons, lettuce, corn, a fresh smoke-cured ham on his new doorstep, etc. And maybe, if a local pharmacist had several children, as did the dentist, service was traded for a running tab at his pharmacy.

Then the government stepped in and said you can't do that. You must set a fixed price and post the price schedule, and a related regulation that *you are not allowed to vary* from that schedule.

And here, essentially, government created a new service business – an eager insurance company selling a dental policy.

Then, some people started getting dental insurance to cover cost. And since the insurance company was paying the bill for some, the prices escalated based on reimbursements.

Today, without good dental insurance, fewer families can afford to have their teeth fixed. Sometimes, they cannot afford it even *with* dental insurance!

And in most communities, most dentists now only

work four days a week.

Of course, with all the new laws, including the ones subsidizing education, insurance and medical fees, costs of educating doctors, dentists, and veterinarians went up, escalated, and continue to increase.

Now, dentist anticipate charging you enough to pay off all their college loans. Quickly.

And because of the increased government-required paperwork, they have to pay for a lot help, from assistants to accountants, and they develop that sense of entitlement to higher fees (like healthcare and politicians everywhere). (As if choice of a profession was solely based on how many dollars they could make . . .)

Surprise! Surprise!

Perhaps, that's why we have some seriously crappy doctors, dentists, and now even vets, out there offering their semi-professional services to mankind and their animals.

With government's encouragement and help, it is all about money for a few, and the control of the delivery system.

It is not so much concern about taking care of people anymore.

It is what happens when government steps in . . .

No one asks, "If government is to protect us, how come we continue to need more of it?"

And no one asks, "If we're getting smarter, how come we need more government?"

So, now, after government forced its nose into the medical tent, the poor (the government helped create, and are creating) can go to a government *free* clinic, and participate in all the other government programs for which they qualify.

You can't expect them to clean out a flower bed or

mow the lawn or take the trash to the dumpster in exchange for their care.

Should there be a safety net? Sure.

It's why we have so many privately-owned insurance companies.

But average workingmen and women, with a little dignity remaining, are forced to pay a government-subsidized insurance company a higher premium, so that other subsidized recipients can line-up at a government-run clinic to get crappy care.

And all we hear is some lying idiot bragging about what they're doing for us.

Read that as "to" us.

And we settle for the 'cronyism' of more State Capitalism, the private-public partnerships between Big Government and Big Business, the new American socialism.

8 wealth vs riches

Is it better to be rich or wealthy?

There is a difference.

You can be wealthy without being rich, and you can be rich without being wealthy.

Both generally look the same in every day outward appearances, which makes the difference sometimes hard to recognize. Most of the time, we are too busy working for a living to care or even remember there is a difference. So, let's look at this difference:

Wealth is that which comes from ownership of an asset, such as a natural resource. Minerals, such as gold, silver, copper, etc., are all natural resources. So are oil and gas, coal, gravel, sand, land and/or water. Precious stones, such as diamonds, emeralds, and rubies, along with such semi-precious stones as topaz, opals, onyx, etc, are also natural resources.

Ownership of "an asset" can economically improve your life...and make you wealthy.

Assets also include the related resources it takes to mine, drill, transport, farm, develop, improve, pump, manufacture, assemble, contain, display, trade, sell or otherwise make use of a natural resource.

Related resources are those things that we can use or convert into products that make our lives better or that others use to improve the quality of their lives.

It is the personal labor, whether it is physical or mental, that man brings to the development of resources that is the origin of property rights.

It is the labor man exchanges in securing or developing assets, that establishes his right to property; to assets. The right of asset ownership, the right of private property ownership, is real - beginning with the life that each individual owns. Another may force the owner into slavery or servitude to reap the rewards of the energy expended; and still others may take it, but the life is never theirs.

Too many are urging government to reduce the assets of others or eliminate their choices for economic and social advancement by limiting the acquisition of assets.

But it is man's work energy, and his creative use of assets and property that improves the quality of his life. The resource may be of a natural kind, or one that eases, or improves the life, or the wants, of man.

But to reduce the ability to acquire assets reduces the value of assets, which reduces the value of our labor and tells us that our endeavors are unimportant.

It implies that we are "tools" to be manipulated for the enrichment of those in control of assets *and our lives*. It artificially reduces the value of some property while increasing the value of other property. It *devalues* the worth of our work and, even more importantly, our lives.

Assets are generally those things which are physical in nature, and have an agreed upon recognizable and consistent long-term value.

Ownership of an asset is an acquired wealth. When an individual gains ownership of an asset, he or she may be on a path to become wealthy, but not necessarily rich.

A wealthy individual may never be rich, but it is unlikely they will ever be completely poor. During the

Great Depression, owners of large tracts of land referred to themselves as being "dirt poor." The term meant that while they owned land, representing a form of wealth, they were not rich.

Riches, on the other hand, are those things that come from or that are generated by ownership of assets; generally, pieces of paper that carry or transfer a claim, or some part of a claim, on an asset. Various currencies, stocks, bonds, mortgages, notes, etc., are all forms of riches.

Acquiring American dollars, for instance, can make you rich when you acquire a lot of them, but they will not automatically make you wealthy.

The value of any piece of paper can change drastically, almost overnight. An individual holding millions in paper, stocks or dollars, can be rich one day and poor the next: Unable to purchase food or shelter, because the value of the currency, or the value of the paper they were holding, has collapsed.

After the end of the Second World War, the people of Germany were holding a virtually worthless currency because of run-away inflation. The *Reichsmark* was worthless as a currency because its value was based on faith in a government that no longer existed. There were no assets providing a value. Many individuals who were holding large amounts of currency were suddenly economically poor.

Ireland, Greece, Spain, Portugal, and many of today's Eurodollar nations, all know first-hand the falling value of their currencies in recent months.

So do Americans, as we watched our government and the Federal Reserve boys deliberately devalue the dollar and set a desired inflation rate of up to 3-percent annually.

But back to the difference between wealth and riches:

The following common everyday transaction serves to illustrate the difference between wealth and riches;

and how each is – or can be – accumulated:

When an individual or a family buys a house and borrows money to finance the purchase, the lender makes a claim on all or part of the property. The lender creates a mortgage (a paper document spelling out the amount of the loan and how the money lent is to be re-paid). Usually, the house is a form of wealth, and the mortgage is a form of riches.

The house is a recognizable, physical asset that should have a long-term value (as shelter is a basic need). The mortgage, as a paper document, represents only a claim on the physical asset and does not have a constant, long-term value.

As the mortgage note is paid, the claim decreases in value; and when the balance is paid-off, is completely without value.

The recent housing crash also shows that an unpaid mortgage can be only worthless paper.

But thanks to our new system of State Capitalism, taxpayers are still forced to subsidize (socialize) by our tax dollars, financial institutions "too big to fail" that were holding these worthless mortgages and other financial instruments.

Of course, these mortgages had nothing to do with the value of the houses they represented. Housing only took the blame for the fast-money boys' shuffling of paper. Their friends in high places could not – and would not – let them take the fall for their wrongdoing, could they?

And millions of Americans, who have taken a bath in some of the recent roller coaster plunges of the stock market, know how the value of stocks (more paper) can vanish overnight.

So, is it better to be rich or wealthy? Of course, the more desirable objective is to be both wealthy and rich. But, the real answer depends upon the economic system in which you live.

If you live in a system offering the freedom of an

equal opportunity to have your choice of economic opportunities, it is better to try and become wealthy.

Assets generally create, and likely will continue, to create wealth.

Accumulation of assets is how man makes progress.

The lack of opportunities to acquire assets is what creates the poorer countries of the world.

Many countries with numerous assets remain poor because the system of government that is in control restricts most citizens' abilities and opportunities to develop the assets.

In an economic system like the one we once had in America, an individual could acquire assets, leading to not only economic self-sufficiency, but also to a path to becoming rich.

If, however, you are unlucky enough to live in a system directed by a few elitist egotists who are primarily concerned with establishing some centralized program (ie; *government partnerships under a capitalistic system)* for economic and/or social manipulation and control (or as they identify it, "the public benefit"), trying to become rich is probably a more desirable short-term option.

This, basically, is because the opportunity to acquire assets is limited.

In order to achieve their national social and economic goals by controlling the means of production, those who make the laws set regulations on how assets can be acquired (with advantages to their families and friends), and artificially set the day-to-day value of a currency, which eventually leads to inflation and a reduction of its long-term value.

The basic problem of a controlled economic system, such as we're developing in America today, is that it eventually creates instability within the economy.

Restrictions on freedom to make economic choices, and an artificially-set value on worthless currency, create predictable waves of instability.

Confidence in one's currency, like the system that governs, must pervade the economy.

When confidence wanes to a point or level of distrust, those in control of the money will create drastic consequences by adding to the currency's instability, which only compounds the distrust and further adds to the currency's instability.

What is an American dollar worth today?

All over the world, people are placing bets on its worth every day.

9 economic wheels, trinkets & trading

Dysfunctional economists and social engineers present models of economic activity as "economic wheels," or "economic motors."

They talk of "world trade" and "world economic forces" and "international trade" as giant motors of economic activity, or as a big wheel turning from one type of economic activity to another type of economic activity, all in a continuous motion.

They argue that government keeps this economic activity going.

They understand the concepts of "government" and "wheel" and "motor." But they forget, or do not comprehend or acknowledge, that from the largest to the smallest, all the wheels and motors must have a "starter" of some kind.

All motors, all wheels, must have a source of energy which starts the turning process.

All motors, all wheels, also need a little bit of grease to smooth the turning process.

When an energy source is consumed, played out, used up, or just cut-off, all movement will eventually cease. This is true for a wheel, a motor, or a human being. When our energy supply plays out, we die.

And if you forget to apply a little grease, bad things are going to happen sooner or later.

Physics, the primary law of nature, and all fields of study except that in the area of economic planners, recognize that all movement, of any kind, only starts when some force of energy is applied. It also recognizes that when energy is cut-off, all movement will eventually stop.

Pragmatically, we know "perpetual motion" does not exist. And therefore, no government can provide it. So, where does this economic wheel, this economic motor, supposedly driving the economy, draw its first impulse of energy?

Any form of an economy, large or small, socialistic or private, developed by government or by any private organization, requires an energy source as a starter. All economic activity begins when one or more individuals exchange personal energy for a basic need for survival purposes: Food, Shelter, Clothing, etc.

A wheel, or motor, only starts turning when energy is supplied by some means.

An economic wheel only starts to turn when fueled by the exchange of an individual's energy for the individual's gain.

As more individuals expend their energy for individual gain, the larger and more powerful the economic motor becomes and the faster it turns. It is this source of energy, multiplied millions of times, that keeps the economic wheels turning.

Crime enters society when an individual, or a group, finds it easier to steal or consume the products — the labor — of others. And as long as the pain is easier than the labor, some will engage in some form of criminal behavior. It is only when the pain for the crime exceeds the effort of crime that the tendency towards crime will be reduced.

This is why society creates government: To use the power of the total society to protect property and life and to punish wrongdoing; the basic grease that keeps things working smoothly.

When those making the laws start to share in the spoils of wrongdoing, of benefitting from crime, the grease disappears and the friction eventually tears up the system, and the individual members of the society suffer...

The question now becomes, are those who make the laws today benefiting from the laws they make or the positions they hold...?

If your answer is "yes", you know something is wrong.

If your answer is "no" or a "don't know", you need to ask yourself if you know of a "poor" politician after they've served three or four terms in office-? (If you can think *Clintons* and still can say "no", when you look in the mirror you will see a liar or another fuzzy-thinking regressive looking back at you.)

Individuals first exchange energy for the basic needs for survival.

Just like our ancestors, we exchange energy for personal wants, such as a greater variety of food, better shelter, protection against real or potential enemies, etc. After fulfilling the basic needs of survival, it is in the wanting of more that the individual starts to accumulate assets, which can generate wealth.

After acquiring an asset, an individual may trade, or barter, one kind of asset for another. When assets are too large, too wieldy, or permanently placed, smaller portable tokens, representing a value of some kind, are used as symbols of the value of assets. This is the reason gold became world-recognized as a desirable medium of exchange.

Different sizes of gold tokens, based on their content of gold, represented various values based upon its relatively stable, consistent and recognized value.

Paper money that represented a claim on gold,

backed by the gold itself, eventually became a much easier way of transporting and trading ownership of assets as it weighed less, and as a same size of paper could represent various amounts of value.

Currencies backed by a gold standard have always been desirable; currencies not on a gold standard have collapsed and disappeared, as they have always come to represent a zero value, worthless in fact and in value.

As organizations, both governmental and/or private, distance themselves from the creativity of an individual's expenditure of energy (for the gain of something with personal value to that individual) rigidity enters into economic activity.

This rigidity comes from the controls, the laws, rules, mandates, and policies, put into place to eliminate any "wobbles" that may start within the system (the economic wheel.)

The farther a society or government gets from the trading of individual energies for individual assets, the more the "wobble" in the economic wheel increases.

Each of us has an occasional "wobble" in our individual systems.

We have days when we are sick, and unable to work. There are days at work when we "feel lucky", and days when nothing seems to go "right". And while they may be important, or even of concern, to the individual they are happening to, they are but tiny "wobbles" in the overall scheme of things.

We need the "wobbles" to make corrections within our individual systems, to spur our creative impulse, to help prevent boredom, and provide us the thrill of our journey on our emotional roller coaster. Otherwise, how would we know joy, sadness, regret, contentment, and all the other things individuals share under a common humanity?

It is from this sharing of humanity that we voluntarily try to establish a means of obtaining common goals and objectives.

But each new governmental regulation of society affects the life of most all individuals, as some responsibility for each personal decision, some freedom to act or a degree of choice, is swapped for some *perceived* common good or public benefit.

But a perception is not a fact.

Individuals form governments to bring structure to a society: To establish common rules and acceptable modes of behavior. A little bit of grease will help keep the wheels running smoothly.

But without reins, or checks, government, which always seeks control, becomes big and powerful; eventually becoming the dominant force in the society that created it. The more control government seizes, the more serious are the consequences of its actions. From too much control come dictatorships.

"Wobbles" appearing in the rigid structure of a government are of a great concern to those in control.

"Wobbles" affects the power of control given to the administrative bureaucrat or bureaucratic office in charge. Anything that cannot be controlled is a threat to the administrator or office – therefore, more controls are needed just to control the threat.

As each "wobble" creates the need for more control, and more control is empowered, government becomes even more structured, more rigid.

Individual energy starts the economic wheel and keeps it turning. But governments see a need to control the economic wheel, as this is the easy way of controlling the individual, those pesky "wobbles".

Under government control however, "wobbles" in the economic wheel can increase to a point where the entire system may collapse.

This economic collapse is what happened with the socialist dictatorships, and the "communistic experiment" of centralized governments in various countries of the world that have tried or are trying to control the means of production.

Entering the new century, we heard American corporations bragging of "getting leaner and meaner", which we have learned is code for "we're cutting jobs" and "reducing dividends".

In our hearts, we know they really are saying, "we're not making enough money" or "we're really going to put the screws to you this time."

Today, while paying multi-million dollar bonuses to a few key executives, they claim they are "cutting jobs and reducing dividends in order to survive".

We hear politicians promising to reduce the size of government and its role in our private lives, while enumerating things that requires an expansion of an existing program or another new program. Generally, what they are espousing are things we do not need or cannot afford, but that will increase the size and power of government.

All we are hearing is an echo of the same nonsense we have heard for over fifty years. A period in which government departments and agencies became bloated and the federal budget increased to over a trillion-dollars annually – and the public debt exploded.

We not only allowed government to become the dominant force in our lives . . .

. . . we voted for it!

Today, we see the money-handlers playing with interest rates and watch them argue over inflation and deflation, and who gets what, while our economic lives fall through the cracks in the foundation.

And those we elect can only promise more of what many are already suffering from.

The results of State Capitalism are where transactions work by A plundering from B the goods of C, and for compensation, B picks the pocket of D of money belonging to E. As the Devil's Dictionary states, "It is an ingenious way of obtaining individual profit without any individual responsibility."

And all of it blessed by a government with a sole objective: the eventual plunder of all the assets of A, B, C, and D, and the total control of the lives of their children and ownership of their children's children.

Today, we hear so-called experts and our elected leaders spouting theories on why Americans have "economic anxieties;" why we have a "spotty economy;" why "people are having a hard time making ends meet;" why "family incomes remain stagnant; why there is "inequality"; and why we have so many "lost jobs."

What they are really saying is "there is a wobble in the economic wheel and we don't know why..."

The same ignorant thinking that got us in this mess will not get us out.

When you sell out to the crooks, the crooks are not going to change the way they do business.

What we do not hear, have not heard, is real talk of how to achieve economic freedom for individuals. Could it be that we have gotten too far from the basic human energy support for our economy?

Is it because we are ignoring the value of assets?

Is it because we are creating a few special people who benefit from a government no longer acting to provide equal treatment under the law?

Is it because it is far easier to control people who are working in a few industries for less and less money, and growing more and more dependent upon the promises of government?

Surely, there must be a reason why we are working for money without any recognizable value?

Shouldn't we be asking, "What are we trading our energy for...?"

To exchange, or trade, a great amount of energy for an asset of little value is, obviously, a waste of energy.

Especially, if the same amount of or even less energy can acquire an asset of a greater value? In modern parlance, we would call this "using your time wisely."

Everyday each of us, to some extent, voluntarily spends energy on non-productive pursuits. But that is our decision.

What is not our decision is that, today, economic opportunity has been reduced to the fact that people are forced to work at "jobs" in exchange for a "wage."

Some of us are under-employed, or in dead-end jobs. This is what we're being offered by government, it is all we have for an equal economic opportunity. But, in fact, it is the death of opportunity.

And at the same time, we are forced to support growing hordes of bungling administrative bureaucrats telling us that it's for our benefit.

Regardless of what we are doing or are trying to do (in exchange for our energy), our government forces us to accept dollars that, basically, are without much value. And what little value they have becomes less every year.

From history books, we know that the early newcomers to America traded "trinkets" to the Indians for assets (land, furs, etc.).

They even traded a handful for some island that is now full of progressive zombies willing to vote for whoever will promise more trinkets, such as a couple of Charlie Sleezeballs.

They have never discovered that size has nothing to do with who can tell the biggest lie.

It is an island of trinket-lovers voting for those pushing trinkets and selling trinkets and buying trnkets.

A trinket is a thing without value: It is a bauble, a cheap piece of ornament, gewgaw, a whim-wham, knickknack, bagatelle, trifle, toy, token, plaything, etc.

An asset is anything that is likely to hold its value,

increase in value, or be used to develop, expand, generate, or produce another asset; today, we are forced to trade our energies for trinkets described as "cash dollars."

Sadly, the American dollar of today is nothing more than a trinket.

It has no recognizable value; as it is not backed by gold, silver, or any kind of asset. Its value depends solely upon the whim-wham of politicians. It is a token, a plaything, of government.

What kind of standard, or "value," is there in the empty promises of a government whose priorities change almost daily?

With its value based solely on our "faith in government," what else could describe the dollar except "trinket"?

In May, 2003, a deliberate political decision by then President Bush and his economic advisors, saw the dollar lose 20-percent of its value. In one month, 20% of the value disappeared – in a deliberate, naked loss of value for the dollar.

This action was heralded by the government expert's excuse that it would "make our products cheaper in world markets".

While this might have been good for a few multi-national corporations, it meant a reduction in what the American consumer could buy for his dollars; a loss in effective family incomes, and a tragic situation for millions of retired Americans on fixed incomes.

And we followed a Bush with an Obama, and a Congress with a same party majority, who plunged us even more into a morass of more debt and more spending, thereby increasing the specter of more rapid and even higher inflation.

As our dollars are without the support of an asset with value, we are at the mercy of gutless wonders acting in their own best political expediency.

The value of our dollar depends solely upon

politicians willing to sell all principles to the highest bidder; crooks who will do anything for a short-term profit.

The dollar is a token, a plaything, of government leaders who will do anything to stay in power. What kind of standard, what value, can be assigned to the empty promises of a government whose priorities change almost daily?

What kind of "good faith" can you have in the value of a dollar when its value can change overnight?

Today, investors all over the world are betting on the value of the American dollar.

What value does our dollar have when government can say, "the value of the dollar is what we say it is..."?

Most of us happily exchange these "cash trinkets" for other trinkets.

Foolishly, we're trading our energy for these "cash dollar" trinkets and trading them for other trinkets, i.e.: Cars, furniture, appliances, TVs, and other things that can only lose value. Most of us completely waste our energy for such things as costume jewelry, the latest fashions, and other objects of glitter and glow, which have no determinable value.

These things are not assets, but things that quickly lose what little value they had...

We buy and horde trinkets because we have been taught that owning them is the "American Dream."

Sometimes, we do acquire some assets: The American Dream was based on the acquisition of assets: own our home or a business of some kind, or a tract of land, a higher standard of living acquired by an accumulation of dollars that represented set, recognized, consistent, and long-term value.

The American Dream was the knowledge that an individual could trade his or her energy for an asset of their choice.

By acquiring enough assets, he or she could meet basic needs and satisfy a great many of their individual wants and aspirations, and have something leftover for their children.

In America today, we are a society of people who are trading our energies not for assets, but for trinkets. We have a whole economy based on trinkets.

We have a nation of Big Banks that will loan on trinkets (cash-flow loans), but not on assets.

Bankers and people in government and people who ought to know better, not only have allowed this to happen, but they have actively participated in a change that is forcing too many of us to live under economic bondage.

Most of us have the ability to acquire some assets. But those in control have declared assets worthless by a policy where only paper (cash-flow) has value. This policy limits economic opportunity to only those who already have money.

Our only choice is limited to trading our energies at jobs provided by others in exchange for dollar "trinkets."

For individuals, assets which have the capability of generating cash-flows cannot be acquired by the use of a small bank loan anymore: Banks will only lend on "trinkets" such as cars and other consumer-type items that cost money, but that do not create assets or even "make money".

And business loans are reserved for lending on money (cash trinkets) itself or huge multi-million and multi-billion dollar loans to monopolies or conglomerates.

Millions of us in jobs, working in a variety of endeavors, are trading our energies for trinkets.

We wonder why we are not making economic progress; politicians wonder why the voters are angry; the talking heads in the news media don't understand what is going on; and the economic experts wonder why the economy is "spotty."

The wonder should be, why are we all wasting our energies on trinkets?

As someone once said, you can sell Americans anything as long as it has nothing to do with the truth.

10 banks vs economic opportunity

There is a myth, like many, that says, *"Once upon a time"* there was a friendly neighborhood banker, and it was his business to know his community and the people in it. This banker was in charge of a limited local monopoly, licensed to provide a community-wide system for local economic progress.

Only the myth remains from those long-ago days.

The myth is similar to that of the family farmer; the tiller of the soil, the producer of our daily bread, the food supplier to the world.

The terminology we still hear, but the family farmer has disappeared under the grindstone of the large agribusiness corporations.

The American farmer sold his soul, his birthright, during FDR's "New Deal," to the federal government in exchange for a guarantee of money not to grow certain crops. It sure sounded good: "Gee, *the government* will pay ME for growing certain crops and also pay me for not growing certain crops."

But along with all the *government payments* came a few controls, including what the farmer could grow, how he was to grow it, how much he could grow, and what price he could sell it for...

The farmer got the subsidies, and the government got control.

But if you can control it, does it matter who owns it?

The American farmer exchanged his private property rights for a government program of crop price supports on a sweeping variety of agricultural products.

We know today, that the family farm is disappearing because of this, swallowed by large corporations with specialists who know how to milk subsidies for maximum taxpayer dollars.

Now, your friendly neighborhood banker has fallen into a similar trap.

Local, independent community banks are mostly gone; swallowed by a few larger banks. Today, the local banker is under the control of the Federal Reserve Board, a flunky in a money supply system that benefits only a few.

Too many banks are not local banks: They are only a branch of a much larger bank in a much larger city in a far away state. The purpose of the branch is not to benefit the local community, but to act as and ensure a conduit for local deposits to the main bank.

The large banks use these funds to underwrite their investments in government securities, stocks, bonds, and other financial instruments. Any loans made are primarily for franchise and chain outlets, international conglomerates and to the friendly, overpaid CEO's of other firms.

To assure this conduit of funds, the big banks tell the local branch banks how they can lend, how much they can lend, to whom they can lend, to whom they cannot lend, and to whom they must lend.

The big banks, without local representation, have little capability to ascertain the local credit needs or how to provide for those needs. There is too little or no local accountability adequately supporting the community.

And, waaaaay too often, too many of the big bank branches located in small cities *are not independently examined* by the banking regulatory authorities, the

Federal Deposit Insurance Corporation or the Comptroller of the Currencys.

This happened because too many community bankers sat idly in the political arena, trusting the politicians they had helped elect to look after their economic interest. Unfortunately, a few greedy large bankers with deep pockets and inflated egos purchased the politician with larger cash donations, in exchange for a guarantee against failure and a guarantee for personal profits.

Many community bankers, thinking themselves financial wizards, wanted to play with the big boys, and they were short-sighted supporters of the big bank's programs. Many of these financial heroes now are financial bums working for a large bank.

For years, local community banks provided funds that created investments in assets and resulted in savings. In doing so, the banks kept numerous small communities vigorous and vibrant. It was what banks did...their reason for being.

To secure a banking license, bank organizers had to show and prove a need in its area for services and financing.

Banks had to show that they would provide local businesses and other local community development endeavors a means of making relatively long-term type investments that provide for local jobs and economic stability.

Present lending policies of our banking system only allow the smaller local banks to provide money for consumer loans or to buy government debt instruments pushed by the banking authorities.

Small businesses with solid and worthwhile assets have a hard time showing sufficient cash flow to satisfy loan requirements based strictly on cash flows.

The big banks, with a few big cash-flow clients, retained for themselves the ability to make big loans to these clients and to friendly investment and hedge fund managers.

These lending practices are those that will hopefully generate double-digit growth for themselves and their investors; and not to help businesses, especially, small business.

Today's loans are mostly short-term investments, and in markets that can panic or overreact. By their nature, they send the wrong signals and create instability in currencies.

Solutions to economic instability lie in local communities, not in placing bets on global economies and foreign currencies.

Current banking practices, with full governmental approval, create a very unequal division of rewards between people who have money and the people who have productive uses for it.

Banking came into being as a means of mobilizing the idle balances of the economy: Those who had money would lend the excess to those who had a likely idea and a need for money to carry it to completion. Bankers acted as intermediaries between those who had it and those who had a worthwhile use for it.

We have lost the idea that any honest and sound undertaking likely to pay is worthwhile.

Banks today are not banks.

They are large corporations that lend to other large corporations for refinancing, for re-payment of debt, for leveraged buy-outs, takeovers, mergers and other cannibalistic purposes. Anymore, banks are only the keystone to a national corporate welfare system; established because of the political demands of a few monopolies, backed by campaign contributions.

There is no ethical reason why economic pain should be forced on many for the benefit of the few.

Why are our national economic policies set to serve just the opportunity for one economic segment?

There is nothing wrong with big-name banks, brokerages, pension funds, insurance companies, and wealthy individuals scouring the globe for legal and Constitutional ways to make more money.

That is justifiable, as it is the name of the game.

It is a high-stakes, high-risk game, and Big Business requires Big Money. But it should not be the only game in town. Why allow only a few select players economic opportunities from the dollar deposits of millions of Americans?

Common sense tells us that if a more assured return on money invested at a lower risk is available, we should take it – if we want to keep our capital.

But isn't it *the degree of risk* that largely determines the difference between a good investment and a bad investment?

Unfortunately, in money circles there is only one game in town. You must be a participating "high risk" partner in order to have an invite to sit at the table.

The only economic segment allowed is cronyism. . .

In smaller local communities, financial institutions do not provide for lending that is an asset-development investment.

Slavish politicians to large campaign contributions treat asset formation and its related savings as a *not-worthy national economic goal* when, in fact, it is the only segment that can underwrite long-term, national economic prosperity and stability.

What we have as economic opportunity today is a government that offers us *promises* of job creation and a $750 billion economic *stimulus program* or a few *tax credits.*

The politicians sweeten the deal with other promises of more expanding government programs for a few subsidized segments and, under the much-abused term of *fairness,* a host of expanded government administrative rules. Then approve a growing national deficit disgrace, and give their permission for the banks to offer us a 19-to-23%-interest rate on our consumer credit cards.

As long as individual citizens are limited in the acquisition of real assets, the gap will continue to broaden between the rich and the middle class; to widen the dangerous disparities between the rich and the poor.

Present lending practices will ensure that economic equality will continue to decline and economic inequality will increasingly divide us.

The only way to change the path we're on is to provide those willing to take the responsibility for individual efforts to acquire assets with the opportunities to engage in a full range of economic ventures.

At local levels, development of assets and savings is hog-tied andstrangled by economic and political strings. These strings lead directly to the corridors of State Capitalism, the partnership controlling narrow national economic policies.

For instance, in February 1995, when the Mexican peso was rapidly falling in value as inflation was near a panic situation, the U. S. agreed to a $52 billion rescue plan for that country's financial base.

In truth, it was a rescue of a few large American investors.

Before 1989, there were limited foreign investments in Mexican stocks and bonds, and only a limited number of direct investors putting money into hard assets such as businesses, factories, land, resorts, etc.

But by mid-1994, almost 75% of new money going into Mexico was coming from American financial centers investing in stocks and bonds portfolios, such as the "tesobonos." These investments were desirable because Mexico's interest rates were showing a much higher short-term yield than rates in the United States on the same amount of money.

But at the end of 1994, Mexican public companies

had $53 billion worth of debts – bonds known as "tesobonos" – of which, $30 billion (over half) was held by American investors and Eurobonds from the Common Market.

Under the January 1995 agreement, the first $20 billion in the $52 billion rescue plan was dedicated to retiring $15 billion worth of the "tesobonos" – because nearly $30 billion of the outstanding bonds were in the hands of American investors.

In February 1995, Gemex, a Mexican bottling company of Pepsi-Cola, rolled over, renewed, $40 million of commercial paper at a yield of 18.125 percent for six months. A New York-based firm of the Weston Group managed the sale of paper for Gemex.

The Bank of New York helped construction company Grupo Mexicano de Desarrollo SA arrange $250 million worth of Eurobonds. Grupo deposited $10.4 million with the bank to cover payments (just over 4-percent).

This was all short-term unsecured debt, which a semi-reasonable individual would call a "high risk" investment. But, remember, there is no risk to large wheeler-dealer investors. They make tremendous sums of money from big up-front fees, with the total of their investment guaranteed by our government.

A government that eliminated the making of small asset-based loans in smaller American communities is now guaranteeing billions in loans by large banks and other financial institutions in foreign countries where they wouldn't drink the water . . .

In a world of global economies, world finance and international markets, there will always be massive economic emergencies, all always chocked-full of surprises. Especially, in a world where currency values are based on faith and hope, and more promises of more baloney tomorrow.

Many (most) of the world's countries are under some form of centralized, un-stable socialistic government.

The United States must be accountable for our own actions, including the value of our currency.

Here at home, these present economic policies will continue to make things worse, for three basic reasons:

First, the only base for our dollars' value is a faith in our government. A "faith" rapidly diminishing in direct proportion to the increasing special status accorded a few privileged conglomerates.

Second, we have let our banks' lending policies kill asset-based loans, the foundation for savings and investments. Banks no longer make asset development loans to credit-worthy people of moderate means: the average individual and American families likely to pay the loans back.

Unfortunately, banks are no longer banks as originally intended. Today, banks are buyers and sellers of stocks and bonds and other companies, and investors in strange financial instruments and weird paper.

Third, lenders and investors are not accountable for their bad judgments, as taxpayers have been (and are) forced to subsidize (socialistically support) their risks of failure.

Supposedly, there is a "risk" in any investment. But it is not always a virtue to make "high risk" loans, even for what some politicians see as a useful political economic purpose.

A creditor should make a judgment whether a particular company or country or an individual has not just the potential and the ability, but the willingness to repay all monies borrowed.

Creditors are the professionals in the financial field, and they should be responsible for their judgment of an endeavor's potential and the borrower's ability and willingness to re-pay. So why are average citizens forced to guarantee – or *socialistically support* – the bad judgment of a lender with the "adjustable rate" interest loan?

Bankers and lenders in general are supposed to be the experts in money matters. But the "adjustable interest rate" takes away the responsibility for a lender's bad decision and drops it on the consumer. By taking the risk, it also creates a policy that encourages inflation, as lenders seek the highest possible return on loans.

Only a complete economic idiot – or a socialist – would argue that the adjustable rate mortgage was not the single greatest reason for the collapse of the nation's housing market.

Individuals and small business people have few if any guarantees against failures in their endeavors.

So, why is there a guarantee to a few large banks and institutional investors against failures? Where is equal treatment under the law in this?

Banks seldom make loans to the home buyer unless the loan is guaranteed by government: They act as brokers, collecting up-front fees and fees for servicing the loan.

For the last 20-years, mortgages up to (and over) a million dollars have been guaranteed by the Federal Housing Administration.

Why are taxpayer's dollars solving an affordability problem for people buying $250,000 to $1,000,000 homes? These people need subsidizing the least.

Politicians allowing the new "financial institutions" to replace asset based loans with a "cash flow loans only" policy, and replacement of loan limits to no limits, and the "adjustable rate" mortgages, are responsible for America's economic problems, and they are keeping America in economic trouble.

Bank regulators declared many small local community banks, with solid deposits and sound capitalization ratios and with healthy asset-based loan portfolios, insolvent – when politicians allowed the

Federal Reserve Board to declare that assets were without value.

These regulations were at the decree of the Federal Reserve Board, made up of private big banks holding billions of dollars in worthless debts.

This change in lending policy declared assets, and the process whereby average citizens of moderate means could accumulate assets, worthless; without value.

Loans for asset-based goods and services were eliminated to reflect a perceived value from the manipulation of paper documents.

Today, we have about 4,500 banks in the United States. A few years ago, there were over 17,000 banks.

Today *91% of the combined assets in all **banks** are* in fewer than 900 banks.

The remaining 9% of the combined assets of all U. S. banks are in independent institutions or small holding companies with assets of less than $250 million.

There are thousands of worthwhile small communities with a total appraised value of less than $250 million.

The Federal Reserve Board, the Federal Deposit Insurance Corporation, the Office of the Comptroller of the Currency, and the Office of Thrift Supervision, all define small banks as *"independent institutions with assets of less than $250 million or institutions with less than $250 million in assets that are members of holding companies."*

Members of holding companies... *are independent institutions?*

Historically, banks were restricted *(not regulated)* financial institutions and, as such, were required to demonstrate that their deposit facilities served the convenience and needs of the communities in which they were chartered to do business, and that the convenience and needs of communities included *the need for credit as well as deposit services.*

Today, as regulated *(not restricted)* financial institutions there are no penalties for non-performance or poor performance, as the national firms claim a "unique relationship" with their subsidiaries and affiliates and their parent corporations.

There are no banks anymore.

All we have are a few financial institutions acting, with the blessings of our elected socialists, as parasites on the economy.

11 *hearts and minds . . .*

"Socialism, like the ancient ideas from which it springs, confuses the distinction between government and society. As a result of this, every time we object to a thing being done by government, the socialists conclude that we object to its being done at all. We disapprove of state education. Then the socialists say that we are opposed to any education. We object to a state religion. Then the socialists say that we want no religion at all. We object to a state-enforced equality. Then they say that we are against equality. And so on, and so on. It is as if the socialists were to accuse us of not wanting persons to eat because we do not want the state to raise grain."— Frédéric Bastiat, **The Law**

Today's "Progressives" call those who believe in Constitutional constructs and restrictions against an all-powerful central government 'extremists'!

That's so judgmental . . . (Sarcastic humor.)

Supporters of our Constitution, Conservatives, Constitutionalists, aren't going to win hearts and minds until we win the "War of Words".

A realist knows there is not any real significant

difference in the political philosophy of President Obama, and key members of his administration, and U. S. Senators like Charles Schumer, Diane Feinstein, *Barb-wa* Boxer, Harry Reid, Susan Collins, – and a House full of Representatives, such as Sheila Jackson Lee and Peter King. Nor, is there three drops of difference on issues between these weirdos and the Democrat candidates for President, Honest Hillary Clinton and The Bernster, Bernie Sanders.

But the progressive regressive socialists are entrenched in both major political parties. Bunches of those in both parties are just illogically dumb enough to think that more government can cure the problems that government has created.

The only ones more dangerous are the know-nothings who vote for them.

They, and the whole sorry bunch of majority voters starting in Maryland and running up the Northeastern Seaboard, along with the brain-damaged voters in Oregon, Washington and California on the Western Seaboard – and Hegel, Hardin, Karl Marx, Joe Stalin, Adolf, Chairman Mao, Castro, and all the others who believe in socialism – are the *extremists.*

There must be something in the water . . .

Today, the danger is that Democrats are democrat socialists and so are the Washington Establishment Republicans.

They are pushing a dead horse that has never worked.

Washington Republicans, the Party moderates – who lean left when they walk and when they talk, pitch "peace" among the "factions" and "bipartisanship" and "moving to the center" – are whining up the wrong tree.

The results of a half-mind baked in its own brand of cowardice.

They do not have the political will to do what is necessary.

Demanding that conservatives join with the socialists in destroying the greatest economic system the world has ever known, and in turn, the greatest nation the world has ever known, is beyond plain stupidity and is completely incomprehensible.

First, the center keeps moving to the left.

The distance from the center to an all-powerful central government, wanted by the socialists, keeps getting shorter and shorter. 50-Years of moving to the center got us to where we are now – in one hell-ova' mess.

As with everything else the left does, what they tell you they are concerned or irritated about is not where it ends.

Washington Republicans are the only evidence of "strife" among conservatives. Indeed, out here in the hinterland, on the principles of less government and more individual freedom there is *near* unanimity.

The "strife" comes from separating the conservative sheep from the Washington goats.

For example, the rapidly-expanding conservative agreement to enforce the Constitutional guarantee of equal treatment for economic opportunity. Conservatives want to stop the cronyism of Big Business and Big Government socialism by (a) a change in law that returns asset-based lending policy to banks or (b) a law that creates small *locally-owned banks* offering asset-based lending for new business startups and economic development endeavors within their local community.

There is universal agreement among conservatives on appointing only judges who fully understand the constructs of our U. S. Constitution, *and will uphold them!*

It is a no-brainer that conservatives want, as it is a guarantee by the Constitution, (1) limited government in all areas of their lives, and (2) protect and promote equal treatment and equal economic opportunities for all under the law.

There is agreement among conservatives on an ethics overhaul, and a litany of other measures ranging from tax relief to education reform to protecting small businesses.

There is agreement that conservatives demand that elected officials live under the same laws that the average citizen lives under. . .

And there certainly is agreement on "no war that we don't intend to win".

Michael Quinn, Founder of the Internet website *EmpowerTexas.com*, once said, "There are essentially only two "'factions"': the vast majority of Republican voters, and a small group of legislative obstructionists who wear elephants on their lapels while acting like donkeys."

What these donkeys described as "strife" is just the righteous indignation of conservative voters tired of the lies of their elected employees and the drift into Socialism because of our elected politicians ignoring Constitutional mandates.

The "peace" party officials want conservatives to embrace is one in which we reduce our expectations, and stop pointing out that these would-be emperors are ideologically naked.

Not. Going. To. Happen.

Conservatives want serious reforms: reforms leading back to Constitutional mandates. If the GOP wants to be the party of principles, then they need to **stop obstructing** and **start producing** serious, systemic policy reforms.

After conservatives gave control of Congress to Republicans, *conservative voters should not be waiting on table scraps from Washington Republicans.*

The time for excuses is over. No more promises: just actions; and no more Republican progressives posing as "common sense" moderates or centrists.

Do not give us more Bushes, more transitory

Trumps, more Compassionate Conservatives, more Liberal Huggers, more McCain Apologists, or more Rommey Status Quos, etc., *and expect our votes.*

Principle is more important than the socialist issues they're spouting.

"A political party cannot be all things to all people. It must represent certain fundamental beliefs which must not be compromised to political expediency or simply to swell its numbers." - Ronald Reagan

12 links in a chain
(Restrictions vs. Regulations)

Individuals are like the links in a chain.

Too many with obvious socialist inclinations see the government's job as welding all those links together.

Practical folks know that you can pull a chain to where you want it to go, but trying to push it to go where you want it doesn't work. And if you do weld the links together, you no longer have a chain; you have a knobby rod or a funny-looking metal stick with holes in it.

Frequently – and sometimes too frequently - those who fear an all-powerful centralized government are accused of being extremists by some ignorant (in the fact that they don't know that they are) socialists: folks who advocate a regimented society for the common good, and believe that government control over the means of production is a public benefit.

Socialists eagerly seek regulations. They become the path to the control center of the system.

Government relies on force; the might of police to enforce regulations that tell us what we have to do, how to act or behave in ways to achieve the goals it establishes.

It is true, factual, that a lot of individuals have a problem with regulations - those "thou will do this or that or we will put thee in jail" type of thing, but have no problem with restrictions, the "thou shall not" type of thing.

At first thought, there may not seem to be much difference in the two, but words have meanings. Words are important (except in the mouth of some charlatan or snake-oil salesman, who destroys all meanings for selfish personal gain). So it is necessary to look at the difference between a restriction and a regulation.

A restriction is a directive that limits or denies an action of some kind, and there are no exemptions. It applies equally to the whole, not to a part or a segment. Restrictions allow everyone, every individual, a choice, and there are no exemptions. Think of Moses and the Ten Commandants. A regulation, however, is a directive that demands an action of some kind that must be done, but there are always exemptions.

As examples:

A restriction is an across-the-board mandate that denies actions that are harmful to others, such as "Do not steal your neighbor's goat" or any property of others.

A restriction assures a level playing field and provides the same rules for everyone: You can't use your neighbor's property as your own; you cannot create a situation or thing dangerous to others; you cannot deny equal opportunity; you cannot take the ideas, the intellectual property, of others; etc.

Restrictions assure that everyone is playing the same game by the same rules; and everyone gets a chance at the brass ring.

But *a regulation* forces action that does not apply to everyone, but only to a select segment or group:

Think seat belts: Drivers and passengers must

always wear seatbelts, but exemptions are provided for school buses (that transport our children) and public modes of transportation that carry groups of people, and for individuals who can get some doctor to say they shouldn't.

Think tobacco: Both tobacco and Marijuana are weeds, but regulations outlaw tobacco in places where people meet in public but, at the same time, some states allow smoking Marijuana in places where people meet in public.

Think economics: During the 1980's, Congress removed restrictions on the type and kind and size of loans a bank could make, replacing them with regulations that gave unfair advantages to big business and killed off the nation's "mom and pop" type of small businesses, which had been creating over 70% of all the nation's jobs. The regulations stated that the nation's banks use cash flows instead of assets for lending purposes.

This created economic opportunities for established endeavors with an existing cash-flow, but stopped the financing of assets for new startups (new businesses don't have cash-flows until after startup).

For decades, there were restrictions against lenders demanding part ownership of an endeavor in exchange for the financing. In the eyes of the law, this was a practice by "mafia" or organized crime types. But in the 1980s, Congress legalized extortion. They removed these restrictions and replaced them with regulations that allowed formation of "equity" or "venture firms" - which can demand part of the ownership of any endeavor they finance.

Less than 20-years after removal of these restrictions, one of the owners of an "equity" fund was a candidate for President of the United States.

How dumb are we...in a decade, new regulations encouraging a type of criminal activity replaced restrictions against it . . .

In the real world, several economists, who value words and their meanings, saw this basically, as devolving the meaning of "criminal" to "equity firm".

The change, of course, created opportunities for those with money to lend - by allowing them to act as parasites on the ideas and talents of others - but at the same time, the change denied economic opportunities to those who cannot borrow money on assets they own.

These changes from restrictions to regulations traded our nation's Private Enterprise System for State Capitalism - the partnership between Big Business and Big Government, America's new form of socialism.

The results are the recent years of falling family incomes, a widening gap between the haves and the have-nots, job increases are part-time jobs, vacant buildings in too many small towns (where small businesses once created jobs and their assets served as family savings), and average Americans facing less choice and no equal economic opportunity.

Too many regulations - with more loopholes than the tax code - are doing us harm.

We need the protection of restrictions aimed at actions which would do us harm.

Restrictions apply to criminals and criminal-activities and to government (the Constitution is a construct of restrictions on government), and they allow people to live together somewhat peacefully. But regulations are dangerous government playthings that create strife and discord and unequal opportunities by creating special privileges for a select few.

A restriction is not hard to understand, but a regulation creates a complicated system for designated actions.

Generally, demands and loopholes contained in regulations are not easily understood - not even by the legislators who dream them up ("You've got to pass it to know what's in it..."), nor by the attorneys who try and interpret them, and the judges who eventually rule on them.

In short, restrictions do not have loopholes and regulations do. For instance:

Presidential Candidate Donald Trump – a "New York Values" conservative – on Tuesday, October 6, 2015 – said he was a strong supporter of eminent domain. (This is the power to take private property for public use by a governmental unit or even private persons or corporations, even when they are authorized to exercise the function of a public character as under a mantle of being a public-private entity).

There is nothing "politically conservative" about eminent domain. <See "Real Estate Titles..." below>

Note, especially, the "right to dispose of" in the book: the word dispose has a special meaning...because it is none of anyone else's business what we do with our property. It is our right to manage our private property as we see fit. At least, until someone acting under a government regulation steps in and takes away our ownership management right by force. And that is what eminent domain allows.

Eminent domain takes away rights of private property ownership – including the right and power to prevent trespass – and transfers those rights to government or those approved by government.

Without private property ownership rights, there are no individual rights. If there is not a right to private property, you do not own your life.

But isn't it your property?

So, those looking for ways to economically improve your life, be warned: Those pushing eminent domain as a good thing are engaged in some form of State Capitalism (cronyism with government), or are unable to see the end resultss of such actions.

Real Estate Titles and Conveyancing, by authors Nelson L. North and DeWitt Van Buren, was published in New York by Prentice-Hall Inc., in 1927. For years, professional experts in real estate law recognized and acknowledged it as "the Bible" on real estate ownership.

In the book's first chapter, *The Elements of Ownership*, the authors declare that the rights of ownership are

- The right to use and possess
- The right to enjoy
- The right to dispose of.

The right to use and possess the land is the most essential. Without it, the present day idea of complete property ownership could not exist. There is included in this right the power of exclusive proprietary authority to the exclusion of any other person (the right and power to prevent trespass).

But elected legislators, however, pass laws that give government agents authority to come onto your property for a variety of reasons: From such purposes as doing tax appraisals, to check for suspected drug sales, or some potential act of terrorism, all without a warrant.

Regulations – government giving a special few special favors or privileges denied the majority – have created the mess we're in . . .

Yet, there are those who see a regulated, regimented society as a common good; and government control over the means of production as a public benefit.

"The two enemies of the people are criminals and government, so let us tie the second down with the chains of the Constitution so the second will not become the legalized version of the first." - Thomas Jefferson

13 ...privacy is dangerous?

Progressive/regressive socialists are busily making privacy a thing of the past.

In public interviews, committee hearings, Sunday talk shows, and every public venue, Washington socialists moan about the intelligence community's need to protect us from international terrorism.

And they do this while blaming the internet service providers of violating the privacy of individuals as they urge massive violation of privacy by a few Washington elites.

While they blame private corporations, they are busy passing directives and laws that force the same companies to hand over all information they collect from users to the government.

It is not okay.

They should be abiding by Constitutional mandates concerning the guarantee of individual freedom. The First Amendment clearly states that the government cannot force others to work for the government, and we each have the guaranteeing of security in the papers (and communications) of our individual lives.

Destroying individual rights is not okay.

We should be screaming that it is not okay.

Similar to updating your phone or computer, but without your consent, the communication providers and intelligence agencies can upload surveillance bugs that essentially clone your devices. Today, there are applications that copy your emails, record your computer browsing history, tap into your phone and voice mail, and follow you on your phone's GPS system. There are programs that can tap into and activate the built-in microphones, turning them into audio listening devices.

These applications, basically, are malware in the hands of government hackers, can take control of a computer's operating system. These and other hackers can transmit every keystroke, copy and transmit the content of the hard drive and every auxiliary memory device.

The hackers not only can steal your information, but can edit your files, insert their own information and data, use your computer to talk with other computers – or just corrupt the system to their desires.

And there are more applications – apps – developed every day.

Consumers actually spend money to download "apps' – paying for the dubious privilege of receiving some company's online advertising, and being followed wherever they go, regardless of terrain or location.

But our nation's progressive-regressives excuse such actions. When it is electronic spying by private corporations, it is just harmless "advertising and marketing". And when by government, it is the only possible action to "protect America" against terrorists attacks.

These are the same folks who are fattening their wallets from corporate donations, and who lack the political will and mental fortitude to kill our enemies before they can kill us.

It is not okay to kill those who want to kill us, but it

is okay for those without the mental guts to protect us to kill freedom by destroying rights guaranteed in our Constitution?

But if we destroy freedom are we not destroying America?

Individuals should never give up the firewalls guarding privacy. To do so, would destroy those precious guarantees of the First Amendment.

The very idea of snooping on supposedly free individuals violates every single Constitutional construct that restricts infringement on our right to be free from government.

It is not okay for corporations in partnership with government and, especially, the government itself, to place filters on internet traffic to search for keywords that might or might not indicate some planned terrorist action. Especially, as it is likely that some Washington elites will use such approval to seek out and punish individuals or organizations worried about funneling too much power into a centralized government; as proven by IRS abuse of conservative groups.

The danger of government malfeasance is too great.

Destruction of America is destruction, whether it comes from inside or outside our borders.

Or how benign the argument presented –

Internet providers and network managers inspect, track and target vast amounts of user's content...and mobile phone communications. Web crawlers seek out keyword targeted data and information. Your internet service retains the right to capture and keep, and even reconstruct, emails.

All software, hardware, tablets and smart phones are subject to invasion.

Hindering communications is the first step in censorship.

When the filters on internet services, on e-mails, computer networks, visited websites, on phones, and all wireless devices, find a proscribed keyword, a request for copies of all communications of the account holder are triggered, and the account holder becomes the target of government agents.

It is immaterial how innocent or benign the intent behind the keyword. In today's world of an all-powerful government, you are guilty – until you can prove your innocence.

This turns our Constitutional construct backward and upside-down. You are no longer innocent until proven guilty.

And government has a lot more prosecutors and a lot more time to prevent you from proving your innocence. And it uses your tax dollars to do it.

All technological devises are subject to assaults that allow hackers to ransom your device, halt all internet and wireless communications, install a virus or malware, and circumvent most all defensive measures.

Today, almost all hardware – including every server, router, switch, computer, tablet, laptop, smart phone – every device – has a backdoor whereby a service provider and/or the national government can take advantage of it.

And many government agencies working out of Homeland Security don't need a warrant to do it.

And who do you think has the world's most powerful computer network to suck up as much information as technologically possible from satellites in space and cables underground and at the bottom of the sea?

And who do you think has the world's largest, most modern, data storage facility to house all this information?

Progressives whine about national "cyber security" needs, but fail to see the over-zealous violations by the intelligence community, just as they fail to acknowledge violations by the IRS, EPA, ICE, NSA, CIA, and a list of other alphabet departments and agencies.

Our government created over 200 new law enforcement and intelligence units immediately after the 9-11 attack.

Now, there are too many governmental agencies for violations not to occur.

Progressive-regressive socialists are giving the national government permission to destroy individual privacy.

Progressives sell "today's world has no boundaries ... old ways are obsolete ... we live in a world economy ... new knowledge ... government needs ... there are no geographical borders ... ... " and a litany of other slogans that actually are false or have no meaning.

They are selling socialism: selling government as the desired result.

But freedom demands an unrestricted flow and exchange of expression with free and open dissent. Ideas demand exposure and dissemination.

Government control is censorship.

What socialists give the government they, first, must take from the individual.

Law is the last refuge of the scoundrel.

Anyone or any organization seen as a possible outsider will soon be an extremist or a terrorist.

Freedom, like privacy, is a thing of the past.

But when did privacy become dangerous?

14 compassion or stupidity?

Sometimes, it is just damn hard to face facts.

But the Associated Press, in November, 2014, reported on Pope Francis' address to the United Nations where he demanded a *"more just distribution of the world's bounty for the poor and hungry..."*

The Pope told a U. N. conference on nutrition "...access to food is a basic human right that shouldn't be subject to market speculation and quests for profit... It is also painful to see that the struggle against hunger and malnutrition is hindered by 'market priorities,' the 'primacy of profits,' which have reduced foodstuff to a commodity..."

We never want to argue with a religious leader, especially one as powerful as the Pope, but the countries without food – the poorest countries on earth – are those with top-down governments in charge: socialists, communists, fascists, and other collectivists and controlling systems. But the Pope, and millions of confused and misguided others, demand that government should guarantee food to every human.

Governments do not grow food, nor produce other goods; those in control can only control those who do.

Regardless of what Pope Francis - and others holding mistaken progressive ideas - may think, it is competition *for profits* within private markets that provide for the development and availability of food and the other basic human necessities.

The Pope is not a student of history. IF he were, he would know that the Pilgrims found out the hard way that socialism does not work.

When the Puritans landed at Plymouth Rock in December, 1620, they adopted the fore-runner of the socialist principle, 'from each according to his ability, to each according to his need.'

Each individual placed his or her production into a common warehouse and received back only what they needed. Then, after seven years, the surplus was to be divided equally among them.

They survived the first winter with the timely help of Squanto, an Indian who befriended the hapless settlers. But their harvests during 1621 and 1622 were small.

The colony's governor, William Bradford, wrote that its (socialist) philosophy did not work. Healthy men who worked thought it unjust that they received no more food than weak men who could not; wives resented doing household chores for other men, considering it a kind of slavery; and the young resented working for the families of other men.

Bradford wrote in his journal that to avoid famine in 1623, the Pilgrims abandoned their philosophy (socialism), writing: *"At length, after much debate of things...gave way that they should set corn every man for his own particular, and in that regard trust to themselves... And so assigned to every family a parcel of land."*

And what a change this was:

These early colonists, each of whom now had to provide for themselves (grow their own food, cut their own wood, etc.), suddenly became very industrious, with women and children who earlier claimed weakness now going into the fields to plant corn.

Under the new system, three times the amount of corn was planted. Scholars report that by the fall of 1624, the colonists were able to export a full boatload of corn.

And the Pilgrims learned a valuable lesson about socialism and hard work.

Since World War II, researchers have collected, organized, mapped, and reported on hundreds of social, environmental, and economic indicators that analyze quality of life trends.

Billions, if not trillions, of public and private dollars have funded every kind of project experimenting ways to solve the unequal access in different world and national communities to employment, public services, education, lending, and many other dimensions of community life.

Study after study have reported on changing economic, social, and environmental inequalities, and other factors in different populations having different life chances depending on their social and geographic location.

Research has focused on the intersection of place and inequality (including gender, race/ethnicity and economic inequalities) both within and between national and international contexts.

Most all these actions have one thing in common: They call for collective, multiple actions by government.

Most all ignore the fact that the lack of equity, education, basic food and water, shelter, and other needed amenities are the result of government action in those countries where such problems exist.

How can the policies that create the problems solve the problems?

Those calling for *more government* to solve the problem of *too much government* must have an emotional or mental screw loose, or a whole bunch of them. . .

As those long ago pilgrims discovered, a private enterprise system provided the abundant food. And up until America started its unchecked expansion into government programs, the private enterprise system created the plentiful amenities that Americans took for granted, and which were the envy of the world.

There is very little doubt that the non-thinking of current progressive/regressives urges creation of more government control.

Today's shortages in seasonal food categories, swings in fuel prices, market instability, and un-checked inflation are the result of America swapping an economic system that worked for one of State Capitalism, the new socialism found in the partnership between Big Business and Big Government.

Compare the results of our previous private enterprise system with the recent total failure of Russia's Communist communes, and it should be evident to all but the mentally deranged that government control creates human misery and enslavement.

And our nation's economic idiots are pushing for more controls in our current system of State Capitalism.

Progressives likely will not need harps where they're going –

Without competition in the market place for profits, how much food would be available for those living in New York City, Boston, Chicago, San Francisco, etc? Only the whip in the hand of the government overseer can force others to grow their food for nothing...

Socialism creates economic slavery. There is no freedom when government controls the means of production. Freedom cannot exist under all-powerful, centralized governments; ask Germans, Russians, Cubans, North Koreans, etc.

Surely, Pope Francis, who is representing 1.5 billion Catholics, cannot be advocating - no matter how progressive and noble-sounding his argument - control of all the world's food by the United Nations?

That cannot be compassion.

But it is the logical result of his argument for world control of food production and supply.

Unfortunately, such thinking ties into the call for an end to capitalism by 130 environmental groups in 2014.

The combined group, mostly comprised of differently named committees or organizations mostly comprised of same individuals holding multi-memberships in all or most of the organization, issued its Margarita Declaration, presented at a United Nations-backed event to increase civil engagement in the lead-up to a major climate conference. "The structural causes of climate change are linked to the current capitalist hegemonic system," the final draft read.

"To combat climate change it is necessary to change the system," the environmental group declared.

The Pope recently visited Cuba, where vehicles emit over 20 times the pollutants than the vehicles in any capitalist country. The environment is not the concern of Cuba's government. A supply of dependent people under their control is the goal.

The point is this: Today's "progressives" or "liberals" are not progressives or liberals at all: They are sociopathic socialists who actually believe they desire a centralized government, like the one in Cuba, forcing us all to act as they want us to act and to believe as they do (political correctness is an attempt at thought-control, not behavior).

Don't believe it?

Google "sociopathic traits" and be amazed at how it looks like the biography of every liberal politician you've known in your life, and who are currently "serving" in Wonderland, D. C. – and their supporters.

And you'll find the traits profiling a majority of college and high school instructors, all teaching some nonsense associated with Hardin's "tragedy of the commons" or Hegel and Marx's failed philosophies.

Modern "Liberalism" is really a mental illness that is reaching an epidemic status today.

Unfortunately, democracy plays into the sociopaths best skills, which are social. This makes them popular to those who can't, or won't think.

Consider the climate idiots who understand economics as much as they understand science, which is little, if not at all...

These "progressives environmentalist" live on the same planet we do, yet, deny that mankind is a carbon based existence.

You have to wonder what planet they're from . . .?

CO2 levels were ten times what they are today back in the age of the dinosaurs. To date, most of those who study the past can account for the dinosaurs' industrial revolution, and a few of them are sorta' sure that man had nothing to do with it –

And some even believe that the world did not end when the dinosaurs' died.

Progressive-regressives never seem to ever consider the possibility that God or the Mother Nature they worship set things up purposefully. They seldom consider that as man becomes "fruitful" (multiplies) the amount of carbon released into the atmosphere creates more photosynthesis for food production, a naturally warmer climate for hospitable living, even more ice melt for a greater water supply and trees to give us shade (and grasses to give your neighbors something they want you to mow).

And they never consider that, possibly, even if they achieve the very reverse affect they're promoting, it will cause (over hundreds of years) mankind to become *more fruitful* - as their way of thinking means less man equals less atmospheric carbon and therefore less warmth; so man huddles together with woman for shared bodily warmth and the process begins again?

And no. Same sex marriage will not assure survival of mankind.

Not understanding basic physics is the basis for their ignorance.

Did you know that CO_2 is heavier than air? Thus, it doesn't "go up into the atmosphere and form a blanket" as environmentalists claim, but it pools at the lower and cooler points on the Earth's surface.

If you don't believe it, simply lie in your bathtub, put 15-20-lbs of dry ice on an insulated pad on your chest, and let it sublime. If you live, scientists are wrong...as the CO_2 (the heavier element) displaces all the O_2 (a lighter element) from the tub.

Unless voters stop listening to these sociopaths, and start requiring political candidates to have some experience, education and skill requirement beyond being an idiot, the United States will continue to deteriorate.

True compassion wants each and every individual to have an equal economic opportunity to pursue his or her economic choice with a right to be free of government control. The proper role of government is to assure that equal opportunity exists – not to create partnerships that benefit their chosen favorite few.

Demanding government control on the means of production, and allowing government control over the lives of individuals, is not compassion.

It is stupidity.

It is past time to start a very long educational and public communications effort to properly connect the foolishness of progressives to the absolute result of their socialistic, central control beliefs.

15 the real evil

Is this a holy thing to see
In a rich and fruitful land,
Babes reduced to misery,
Fed with cold and usurous hand?
And their sun does never shine,
And their fields are bleak and bare,
And their ways are filled with thorns:
It is eternal winter there.
For where'er the sun does shine,
And where'er the rain does fall,
Babes should never hunger there,
Nor poverty the mind appall.
William Blake - 1794.

Blake tugs at the heartstrings. But we should never forget that government creates enslavement and human misery.

Ask the citizens of Cuba or Argentina. Think Germany and Russia and China and North Korea. Look at Iraq, Iran, Afghanistan, Libya, Syria, etc.

And America is on her way . . .

Kennedy's New Frontier opened the door to more government, and government expanded in Johnson's Great Society to the delight of progressives everywhere. But the numbers are in, and the War on Poverty has resulted in more people living in poverty; the number of poor increased, after spending trillions of tax dollars.

Taxpayers grew the size of government – but the bottom line, we should all know by now, is that governments do not win wars on poverty; they create poverty.

The poorest countries on earth have a centralized government promoting more government power.

But Americans have forgotten that the private enterprise system created equal economic opportunities for everyone, *whereby individuals could economically improve the quality of their lives*; and it created the greatest economic system the world has ever known.

But today, we have exchanged economic opportunity – the private enterprise system – for State Capitalism, a socialistic partnership between Big Business and Big Government. Under this new system, all we have anymore is a welfare program for large corporations, conglomerates, monopolies and the very rich.

Only the brain-dead cannot see that our government has killed or is killing economic opportunity for all but those who have money.

State Capitalism has created – and continues to create – a system of economic and government royalty in our supposedly "classless" society.

But our United States Constitution's Article 1, Section 10, states "No State shall ... pass any ... ex post facto Law, or Law impairing the Obligation of Contracts, or grant any Title of Nobility."

The authors of the *Federalist Papers* argued that the limited Constitution they had just passed contained certain specified authority *exceptions to legislative acts*:

For instance, *"as that it shall pass no bills of attainder, no ex post facto laws and the like. Without this, all the reservations of particular rights or privilege would amount to nothing."*

"There is no position which depends on clearer principles, than that every act of delegated authority, contrary to the tenor of the commission under which it is exercised, is void. No legislative act, therefore, contrary to the Constitution, can be valid."

"To deny this would be to affirm ... that the representatives of the people are superior to the people themselves... "

Alexander Hamilton wrote in the *Federalist Papers: "A Constitution is, in fact, and must be regarded by the Judges as a fundamental law. If there should happen to be an irreconcilable variance between the two, that which has the superior obligation and validity ought, of course, to be preferred: in other words the Constitution ought to be preferred to the statute, the intention of the people to the intention of their agents."*

Again, these principles of limited Constitutional government were restated in 1943, in Jones v Ross, 173 S.W.2d 1022 (Texas): "It is fundamental that the Constitution is the paramount law of the state and cannot be altered by legislative amendments."

And in 1982, the Supreme Court ruled in Loretto v. Teleprompter Manhattan CATV Corporation that "...government does not have unlimited power to redefine property rights."

But government is claiming more and more Imminent Domain powers. Soon, governmental units will argue that their administrative management of private property is a lawful Taking.

The State Land Patent, which binds states to protect contracts of land deeds, is a warrant to the Original Patentee and its assigns and heirs "forever absolute" indefeasible fee simple title *forever.*

These rights in the estate in land include the right of absolute disposition, that is, the right of exclusive management. The accompanying right to prevent trespass makes this right of management exclusive against all others in the world – including government.

The State may not deny its grant of the Land Patent – as it is basic real estate law that the Grantor may not deny its grant.

Therefore, no matter how many "planning" laws a legislature passes, the partisan Hegelian administrative state cannot claim "King's X" to, ex post facto, assert mystical powers to sever (outside the bounds of centuries of real estate law) and then manage the private property estates of free Americans.

The Constitution's 13th Amendment strictly prohibits slavery and involuntary servitudes in America.

Most understand that, in most arenas, the very word "planning" means the *administrative state management of private property* – and the lives of their citizens.

This is the functional equivalent of Karl Marx' centralized control of the modes of private production that abolishes private property, which abolishes equal economic opportunities - the rights of individual freedom.

This means that "government planning" that ignores millions of pre-existing legal contractual relationships may not be legally possible. There should be consequences for such unlawful "planning".

The countries of the world that have the most citizens living in poverty – in misery and enslavement – those with fewer economic opportunities – are countries with a centralized government.

And in today's America, we have too many, who are too emotionally handicapped or mentally deranged to see and acknowledge and understand this fact. They blindly urge more government programs with more government control for America.

No one with a logical mind can deny that what government subsidizes government controls.

Think not? Then, name one government program that does not carry control within it.

Control and freedom are natural enemies.

Before crying for government "to do something", ask what three problems has government really solved?

Aren't most of the things that government actually accomplishes temporary?

And ask, "In America today, how many of our problems are the result of some government action?"

If you apply a Constitutional test of "equal treatment under the law", you will conclude that today's massive administrative police powers of government is our national problem.

Those demanding more government are the real evil in today's world.

16 more government

You usually can spot a Progressive Socialist Utopian regressive as soon as they utter about three sentences.

These wanta-do-gooders do a great deal of damage to the economy by wasting tax dollars, distorting economic activity and by attempting to subvert Constitutional constructs which guarantee the individual's right to be free from government.

Any official who does not honor the public official's sworn oath to protect our sacred Constitutional rights needs to be removed from their job.

Turn those bloodsuckers free to seek other work.

Officials who do not respect Constitutional rights do not deserve respect.

The "common good" is always synonymous with "progressive activism" or, as the progressives, liberals and moderates like to refer to it, the "Human good".

The common or, if you insist, human good, is part of the 'arrogance complex', which supposedly consists of 16 different gates to the labyrinth of evil.

It always falls fatally short of 'Divine good'.

Historically, the arrogance of successful common good activism is overtaken by "criminal arrogance", whereby the activism of the 'do-gooder', results in loss of freedom and property for those whom the common good, supposedly, was to benefit.

Human history is replete with the conclusive evidence: Observe the French Revolution with its beginning in the activism of "the common good" - which was destined to fall to the criminal elements rising up as the leaders of the stupid masses. They assumed the power to celebrate the use of the guillotine as entertainment on France's aristocracy.

This leadership the Revolution spat out eliminated any attempt of due process, which created a thirteen-year "reign of terror".

France has never recovered.

Additional evidence exists in the same or similar arguments of "common good" activists that rewrote the histories of Spain, Germany, Russia, Nigeria, Cuba, Haiti, Argentina, Iraq, Iran, etc.

Not one single leader that the "common good" activists threw-up (literally) in these and other countries became rulers and dictators by promising evil and murderous reigns. In truth, the opposite occurred: each proclaimed they were dedicated to improving the lives of all. Everything they promised was for "the common good".

And wantabee leaders in the United States, declaring and promising they will work for the "public benefit" of "the people" for the "common good" are the most dangerous of all. They lie.

They lie to themselves, and they lie to the voters.

"The common good" – whether sincerely preached by compassionate conservatives or a Democrat socialist – is the path that leads to human misery and economic slavery.

It always has; it always will.

Even the New England ship owners' participation in the slave industry (transporting slaves to the American market) claimed that it was a public benefit and a common good. It wasn't, but it was creating wealth for the owners and their investors.

The arrogance of the "human good" activists is only surpassed by their emotional handicap or mental derangement in wanting to assume guilt for their other short-comings.

One must turn a blind eye to the U. S. Constitution, abandon markets created by private property rights, and then resort to top-down central planning and control of the modes of production to achieve the "human good" desired. And, apparently, accept the socialists' belief that private property rights are a "whim" –

But when you ask the government for help *it ain't going to be free* – someone pays. The examples that comes to mind are the Catholic Hospitals that are being forced to perform abortions ... because they have accepted government funding. Or farmers who are no longer free to plant what they want to go on their own land (because the government pays farmers to grow some crops, but not others).

But progressives – socialists in general – claim that what they are doing is because of scarcity of goods, services, resources or behaviors that need their corrections. And it does not matter if it is food, wildlife, people or rainfall. There's always something missing.

And they seldom ever realize that what is missing is from inside their head.

Progressives apparently have not a clue what science is...the scarcity fallacy is a bit of fuzzy-thinking nonsense, based on the "tragedy of the commons" – an anti-science attitude of scarcity.

But before houses, there was a scarcity of housing; before farming, a scarcity in food and food variety; before steam, a scarcity in ships, trains, cars, and other transportation modes; before electricity, a growing scarcity of whales (whale oil was the world's #1 lubricant).

The *fear of scarcity* is what politician's sell, not scarcity itself.

Today, the greatest scarcity is that of thoughtful common sense.

The fallacy of scarcity is that man keeps creating new ideas and developing new ways of dealing with human wants and needs. We always have, we always will . . . if we can keep government promoters out of our lives.

We pay government bureaucrats and politicians a salary, pay for their expenses and healthcare, and pay for their retirement and, in exchange, they work to place our property – and us – under their control.

How dumb are we?

Dr. John Marini, a professor of political science at the University of Nevada, Reno, observed that in America, the administrative state traces its origins to the theories of the German political philosopher Georg Wilhelm Friedrich Hegel, who influenced Marx. Hegel believed the erection of the modern state marked an "end of History" – a point at which there is no longer any need for conflict over fundamental principles. He believed that politics at this point would give way to administration, and administration would become the domain not of partisans, but of neutral and highly trained experts.

But Hegel's Pollyanna theory did not work out too well, did it?

Following Hegel's Happy Talk, Marx claimed to have removed politics from politics. And that did not work out too well, either, as *politics cannot be removed from politics.*

Except for the politically blind, Hitler and Marx blew Hegel's unbaked idea to smithereens.

In his 1951 publication, *Socialism*, Ludwig von Mises also noted that Marxists' "science" cannot be proved, and neither can their "social" economics.

Today, half-baked Democrat Socialists without borders, and do-gooders and Utopians who think the same way as Hegel and Marx, have no place in an advanced, anti-slavery civilization.

Only the most of the gullible believe otherwise.

It is unthinkable that anyone could turn a blind eye to the scarcity claims represented in "the greater good" – a concept author Ayn Rand uses to warn of the Soviet Union's results in subhuman misery, enslavement and death.

But America's administrative development of civil law is forcing involuntary servitude (in the form of agency regulations that are placing restrictions on centuries of common law concerning private property rights) that has no place under our Constitution.

Forcing controls on individuals and private property owners by questionable and seemingly lawless administrative edicts is a form of involuntary servitudes, which is prohibited by the 13th Amendment – and SLAVERY has no place in a Democratic or Republican political policy platform.

But both major parties, regardless of what they say, keep playing patty-cake with the supporters of more government.

There is no difference in Washington Republicans and Democrats when it comes to doing anything that will help keep them in office.

The current Republican House and Senate leadership refuse to strike sparks in the power structure by demanding an Independent Prosecutor to seek an investigation into the increasing un-Constitutional administrative actions.

And they refuse to pass legislation in fear of a veto by the President, and they would not have enough votes to over-ride it.

It's called cowardice.

And principles simply do not matter to party bigwigs, regardless of what they may claim.

The two-party system does not seem to be working, and things keep getting worse:

According to national polls, a self-described socialist from Vermont, Senator Bernie Sanders, as a Presidential candidate, had the support of over 35% of those who said they were Democrats.

A self-proclaimed Socialist seeking election to be the President of the United States, and he had the support of over 35% of those claiming to be Democrats? And differences on issues among all the Democrat Presidential Candidates were so small they were almost non-existent.

And the Republican Leadership urge their candidates to "move to the center"?

Those who want government in control only want government in control of others. No one is advocating government control over himself or herself, only on the other guy.

It's always the other guy who needs controlling.

All we have are politicians, who shirk from any danger to the position or office they hold, offering themselves as heroes protecting American interest (and Americans), while they enslave us by their actions. It is the behavior of liars and cowards.

Never do they ask, "Who will control the controllers?"

But there are those among them who think they see the answer in the mirror . . .

17 STOCK MARKET FORCES

What stock market forces *prevent* a significant influence on prices?

The question, in itself, carries implications for the policy makers as well as the consumer and small investors.

It observes that what we *are told* - that the market place determines stock market prices – may not be a valid supposition and, in fact, is false.

And it all can be traced back to the origination of the first *"quicksilver"* funds.

Today's high-frequency traders rapidly buy and sell large amounts of securities with statistics and algorithms that drive electronic-trading strategies. They use high-speed data systems, linked with underground networks and locations that are strategically-positioned close to the servers of electronic exchanges, so that they can compete to buy and sell in increasingly smaller fractions of a second.

And their influence is substantial. These high-frequency traders now make up slightly more than *half the daily volume* on all the U.S. stock exchanges.

These traders are high-tech pirates who destabilize the markets. In doing so, they control a free market stock-value exchange for the dollars of most average market investors.

The technology advantage that "high frequency" stock market traders use is real.

Ordinary investors cannot compete with them.

Here's why...

The technological advantages allow the high-frequency traders to spot and capitalize on very small discrepancies in bid/ask spreads among various exchanges. In the process, they drive the wide swings in stock market prices.

Those claiming that this is a good thing include such "average investors" as Warren Buffett, John Bogle (Vanguard founder), former SEC Chairman Arthur Levitt, George Soros, and the board members and executive officers of the world's hedge funds and other huge financial institutions.

But these wide swings in markets are not good things for ordinary investors:

Ordinary investors do not have the necessary funds to afford the technology (and staff) to make million-dollar profits on a half-point or even less fraction spread on a huge volume of stock. When you're buying and selling in billions of dollars, two or three or more times a day, a penny or two on millions of shares soon add up to a huge profit in one day.

Then multiply the days and you're talking about billions and billions of dollars.

And when buying stock in billions of dollars, the public price will always increase dramatically, just as stock prices will always drop when billions of dollars are withdrawn when sold. So, as a big time investor, you want volatility in the market place. And you want to make it happen when you want it to happen.

When this occurs - and you're buying and selling in volumes that will create these price swings – so you know before it happens, *when* it will happen – it's not gambling, and you stand to make enormous profits every day.

It is nothing more than stock market manipulation.

Stock market manipulations are nothing less than rigging the system: A game allowed by politicians declaring that (their partners in) these big financial conglomerates are "too big to fail..."

And the average investor is a sucker; they don't understand or know the game they're in . . . let alone what the rules are.

Today, this technology – controlled by a few huge hedge funds and financial institutions – *prevents* the market place from determining stock market prices. The implications should be terrifying for the policy makers as well as the consumers and small investors.

Especially, when "those too big to fail" now claim that *transitory events* coincide with unexpected changes in prices because the supply cannot change fast enough.

This in itself is a strange claim: It means that consumption has nothing to do with or has no relationship to production volumes, or vice versa, and that inventories do not matter and are not part of the equation.

This is an argument that claims (a) supply and demand has nothing to do with stock and commodity markets, and (b) that only arbitrage affects price, existing only because of market inefficiencies and that it ensures market prices do not suffer wide swings.

Well, maybe. . .

. . .and maybe it is just a lot of baloney from those who have money or know those who do.

A *transitory event* – a known or unknown action – means that a corresponding *transitory shock* must occur in some market variable(s). But historically, the variables were consumption determining supply and demand; not arbitrage.

But describing a *transitory shock* as a *transitory*

event sounds better; it signals more involved and convoluted information and data that only the privileged insider and the mentally superior can understand.

Claims that only arbitrage on transitory events sustains a market (and thereby, stock prices) produces a scary fact: It would seem to provide a motive for the ethically-challenged to make certain that such opportunities occur in the short run, which can present profitable *opportunities* that will support large capital investments.

Especially, if the market price of certain stocks can be, and are manipulated by those who seek to profit from the opportunities of buying and selling of stock or stock equities influenced by a series of these up-and-down *transitory shocks* – or as the big money boys call them, *transitory events*.

For the average investor, such *events* or *shocks* substantially complicates their ability to invest with a degree of confidence in the market place.

The creation of these shocks or events eliminates any elasticity of market demand and market supply as the critical determinant for long-term market stability. (Elasticity in the market place applies to market forces that respond to expected events.)

For years, the price of listed stocks was an appropriate response based on expected or anticipated events of more publicly known factors, where future development and pricing plans were and are common knowledge. It was this elasticity, a reliable give-and-take, which determined prices within the market place, whereas market *shock* or a transitory *event* is a totally unexpected occurrence.

In one easily identifiable industry or market segment a pronounced on-going series of "unexpected occurrences" implies that all the known factors have been removed from the equation.

It also must imply that some other force is at work in the marketplace or that particular segment of the market, which may be a true or false event.

The wide swings in oil prices come easily to mind.

As do the range of excuses.

Over time, wide swings in market equilibrium - based on *market shock* - should refocus discussions to a public examination of the framework of the forces at work in that segment's market environment for trade and pricing.

Claims by those practicing arbitrage that *transitory events* coincide with unexpected changes in prices because supply cannot change fast enough should be suspect. Arguments that consumption has nothing to do with or has no relationship to production volumes, or vice versa, and that inventories do not matter *are implications* that market forces in certain market segments can be and likely are being controlled to some extent.

There is no other logical explanation or conclusion.

If so, these *transitory events* do not represent opportunity as much as they do manipulation.

Our nation's federal policy makers must consider these implications if the stock market is to survive as a viable financial vehicle for the consumer and small investors.

As a nation, we place warnings on tobacco products, drug labels, toys, airbags, etc.; on a whole host of things.

If, as it seems under State Capitalism, the national stock exchanges are becoming merely playgrounds for a few large investors, shouldn't a significant warning be required of that fact and provided all the nation's investors?

To trust today's market forces at work in the stock exchanges may not be wise.

18 QUICKSILVER FUNDS

(This chapter first came to light in our musings of late 1988, written long before the term "hedge funds" came into vogue. At that time, these funds were without a name, and we simply called the process "Quicksilver funds". It was our look into the future and even the word "derivatives" was unknown at that time. Things are worse now than in our view from back then...)

Investors will put billions of dollars into countries where they wouldn't drink the water.

These dollars are known as "quicksilver funds", so-called for their quickness in switching from one type of investment into another, chasing after a higher rate of return. To many who have seen years of families' savings disappear in some of these types of investments, another name for them is "stupid."

Quicksilver funds are portfolio funds, or money invested in paper, and are short-term investments. (Funds invested in hard assets, businesses, factories, land, etc., are known as direct investments.)

Quicksilver funds can be heavily invested in such things as a Mexican peso and the next minute, with a flick of a computer switch, be invested in German marks, the Japanese yen, the Portuguese escudo, or whatever currency or stock is bringing the highest short-term yield.

Usually, these huge amounts of monies do their sudden switches because of inside-knowledge about a planned change in some country's political-economic agenda or on a rumor of political-economic change or some new oil field find.

In their chase from one investment type to another it often means some economic upheaval for the type of investment they withdrew from...

Countries open to international flows of capital sometimes find themselves in economic chaos when spooked foreign investors, for rational or some other reasons, suddenly decide to press another computer switch.

If the investors lose confidence in the nation's economy, or if the opportunities for profit improve elsewhere, quicksilver funds are immediately yanked out of the financial system.

Does this create inflation? It must.

Quicksilver money creates inflation going in, and usually when it leaves.

Whenever you have too many dollars chasing the same thing it creates its own inflationary pressures.

And when quicksilver funds leave, in the space of a few days, a country suddenly finds itself going broke and unable to repay its debt. Under pressure, their national currency nearly always undergoes an emergency devaluation.

The results are much the same with the stock prices of the companies they pursue.

The history of quicksilver funds is a relatively short one. They are a new investment phenomenon, created by three somewhat related events:

First, during WWII, under a national emergency, the government budget exploded with growth. Then, with Korea, Vietnam, and the "cold war," with the social engineering of Kennedy's "New Frontier" and Johnson's "Great Society", government expenditures rapidly surpassed government revenues.

But the United States needed, or so our political leaders thought, to help the "under-developed" countries of the world. But how could they do it?

Taxpayers would not likely take too kindly to shipping their money off to some foreign land. But there had to be a way to do it.

In the mid 1970's, such countries as Brazil, Mexico, Argentina and other countries around the world were desperate for money.

These countries, because of their centralized government systems of bad management, were being ravaged by inflation and governmental unrest. But a loan from ol' Uncle Sammy would keep their governments in control. But Uncle Sam was running a budget deficit, too. And was dealing with some pesky taxpayers who just *would not understand* why their money should prop-up some socialists in some far-off places.

Government planners know that government can do all things. And that government should do all things. And they were convinced the U.S. needed to make these loans. So, the bureaucrats came up with a visionary deal: They would get the American banks to provide the money.

Why not? The banks have all the money, anyway.

Being broke, these countries, naturally agreed to pay exorbitant interest rates, usually 15 to 16-percent, for borrowed funds. There was no way, at that time, for our American banks to achieve such potential high rates of return for loans here at home. So, greed found a way to overcome sound banking judgment.

Realizing that such loans were not likely to be re-paid, the big banks, through their henchmen at the Federal Reserve Board, suckered Congress into making the American taxpayer responsible for repayment when these seemingly bad loans would "go bad."

The big banks, already with too much political clout, went to the social and economic planners acting as "public servants" in an out-of-control government and made a deal: Since the government, already awash in red ink, didn't have money, the banks would lend to the foreign countries *if the government would guarantee the loans would be repaid.*

And "paid for" politicians could not say "no."

Such guarantees would never be placed within the budget process, and any potential losses would be for some future accountability.

A cadre of "departmental servants" descended on lawmaker's offices to "sell" this package for Congressional approval. With the active help of the nation's liberal news media to spread the message, all protests were quietly ignored.

Extravagant amounts of money poured into the coffers of these friendly (and some not so friendly) nations from the vaults of a few large banks.

Using the funds gathered from millions of individual and family investors, like lemmings in their mad dash to the sea, mutual funds, brokerage houses, insurance companies, pension funds, etc., in a search for additional profits, followed the big banks foray into foreign investments.

By the late 70's, these countries were defaulting on billions of dollars worth of loans. The banks, in order to show a profit, and prevent any political fallout, would make an additional multi-billion dollar loan to the countries in default, so that these countries could at least pay the accrued interest. This made things look good: on the books, there were no bad loans, no unpaid interest charges. What actually was going to be a big loss looked like a pretty profit picture.

And the U. S. government was guaranteeing all the loans.

But here at home, interest rates were sky-rocketing.

Why wouldn't they? The banks were getting 15-to-18-percent on billions in loans guaranteed by the central government. If our nation's businesses wanted money, they had to pay a high rate for it.

The rates soared to over 25-percent for consumers and small businesses.

Next, in the mid 1980's, in order to force our government to abide by the agreement for repayment on these big bad loans, the big banks, through the Federal Reserve Board, changed the banking rules.

This change in banking rules created the economic recession of the late 80's and early 90's, and the resulting policies are the main reason for the economic instability in today's economy.

It is also one of the reasons for quicksilver funds. The "big loan syndrome" evolved from the big banks' guaranteed foray into big foreign loans.

In 1975, when banks made asset-based loans, it was almost impossible to find a bank that would make a loan for over $1,000,000. A borrower of this amount and over, sought funds from insurance companies, pension funds and other investors.

By 1980, in five short years, it was almost impossible to find a bank, or any lender, that would make a loan for UNDER $1,000,000.

Banks had discovered that big loans earned big fees.

In the decade between 1975 and 1985, big banks started making big loans to big corporations. The new economic game was corporate takeovers and mergers; multi-million and multi-billion dollar deals financed for big up-front fees.

Those brokerage houses, mutual funds, insurance companies, pension funds, and other institutional investors, who had followed the banks, were now looking for ways to salvage billions of dollars in investments that had gone sour.

New specialists arrived who did nothing but arrange fees for financing corporate takeovers and mergers.

By combining a healthy company with one that is an economically-sick corporation, new stocks, junk-bonds, stock-swaps, and new paper-products of all kinds, could be issued. This new paper promised huge future potential profits.

In less than 15-years, the stock market climbed from around a 1,600 benchmark to over 11,000. This, as millions of families, who had invested in this new paper, lost large portions of their family savings.

In the ten years between 1975 and 1985, assets of many big corporations were mortgaged to the hilt.

Sometimes, with the active help of their accountants and lawyers, corporate assets were mortgaged for two, three, ten times their actual value.

Conglomerates, with multi-billions of dollars in hard assets, were going bankrupt.

Banks and investment funds had to come up with a means to show some short-term profits: A way to keep the wolf from the door.

With their on-going experiences of making big loans to foreign countries, based only on the country's promise to repay with proceeds from their tax revenues (cash flows), the central bankers found their way.

Over-mortgaged on assets, with many nearing bankruptcy, the conglomerates still had money cash-flows based on their daily operations. As the banks held the mortgage on assets, bankers could easily understand that they should benefit from this money flowing through the corporation's daily sales.

The bankers didn't want to foreclose and plunge the nation into economic chaos, but this cash-flow, so they claimed, was rightly theirs. All the bankers had to do was convince their fellow bankers and friends in the Federal Reserve System.

"Look," they more or less said, "we can't lend any

more money on these assets, but we'll lend these bankrupt firms more money, enough to keep them going, based on their cash flows.

"We'll just call assets 'collateral,' and keep them under mortgage, but we won't lend anymore money on them. We will just lend on the cash."

"Fine," say their friends on the Federal Reserve Board; and they then issued new bank regulations and guidelines that declared assets of no value for new investment loans.

And the new order of the day was "cash-flow loans only."

This effectively killed new business startup loans, based on assets.

Asset based lending built the world's best economic system. For almost two hundred years, asset-based lending provided funds for millions of small businesses, created millions of small endeavors resulting in economic gain for millions of individuals and families, created millions of new jobs, and created the greatest number of economic opportunities for the greatest number of people ever recorded in human history.

Asset based lending was the backbone of the American Idea.

It created the economic opportunity for millions of people and provided economic choice. Asset based lending had been the backbone of small businesses; endeavors that created three out of every five jobs in America.

Asset based lending created the world's leading economy, the highest standard of living, and the greatest prosperity for more of its citizens than the world had ever known.

By one stroke of a pen, the Federal Reserve Board, made up of private big banks, wiped out assets as desirable resources; reduced the incentive for savings and investment; killed wide-based opportunities for new small business startups; and opened the door to all sorts of financial wrong-doings.

It declared assets worthless and placed paper as the basis of all value.

But what did this change in lending practices create? What were the results?

Well, ask the families and the retirees about the drastic reductions in the value of their savings resulting from losses in a manipulated stock market. Ask the ex-employees of some big corporations that enjoyed the enthusiastic support of the nation's bankers, mortgage firms and stock-brokers.

Ask those in court for "white collar" crimes involving their years of financial shenanigans. Better yet, ask the wonderful politicians for whom you voted all these years...

Today, we are a nation made fearful because of economic instability.

We are a nation where too many families are falling below the poverty line, as we lose jobs, and most available jobs offer under-employment for too many workers.

We are a nation where young people devalue their lives because they don't see an opportunity for advancement; where increases in crimes against persons and property grows more common; where a lot more people are on street corners washing windshields and selling gum; and too many people are selling dope and guns.

This is too high a price to pay.

The third reason for quicksilver funds is the world-wide drug trade.

Official estimates of illegal drugs' cash-flow into the American economy range from $150 to over $500 billion annually. This is equal to almost a third of our nation's annual Gross National Product, and is all part of a tax-free underground economy.

Some argue that if it wasn't for these billions of drug

dollars, here and abroad, finding their way into our economy, the recession of today would be much more severe.

Beginning with increased usage and sale of illegal drugs in the 1960's, the money had to undergo laundering in some way. As illegal drugs could not be acknowledged as an asset, the dollars were stuffed into suitcases or into boxes hidden in a closet, thrown in the back of cars, and used to purchased a lot of things from unconcerned sellers. Dollars by the billions develop into storage problems. So, what does one engaged in the drug trade do with all these millions and billions of dollars?

One finds a way to make them clean. One finds a way to launder them, a way to make them legal.

Who handles money in large amounts? Banks.

Who thinks every dollar in circulation belongs to them? Bankers.

So, what you do with all those dollars received from drug trafficking is pay someone to clean them, someone who knows how to launder them.

Treasury officials estimate that more than $300 billion in ill-gotten profits is moving through the world's financial system every day.

In 1988, an arm of organized crime, headquartered in Salt Lake City, Utah, purchased a Houston, Texas, area bank; a purchase approved by banking authorities. The bank became a conduit for laundering dirty money. The capital assets were stripped from the bank while millions of dollars of dirty money became clean again.

In 1994, American Express companies, without pleading guilty, paid the Justice Department over $50 million in a "settlement" of a multi-million dollar drug-money laundering scheme involving several accounts at U. S. and Swiss banks and Cayman Island holding companies.

Over $500 billion in forfeitures and another $200

million in civil penalties were assessed against financial institutions stemming from the BCCI fraud and money laundering investigation of 1993-1994. Not one officer in the bank's New York headquarters ever went to prison. One of BCCI's top officials was attorney Clark Clifford, a long-time Democratic Party advisor and a close friend to former President Lyndon Johnson.

Since 2010, after the bailout of banks "too big to fail", over a dozen of the nation's largest financial institutions have reached "settlement agreements" – totaling over $30 billion dollars – with investigators. How many of these "settlement" dollars have actually been paid is unknown...

Since 1995, more than five hundred money-laundering investigations have been conducted; (dozens involving American and Mexican financial institutions). There are thousands of suspected drug-accounts in hundreds of foreign banks and investment firms.

Investigators claim that international bank-secrecy laws hinder their efforts to accumulate financial data for examination.

As billions of dollars of dirty money move through the world's financial centers, our banks, our financial institutions, our brokerage firms, our drug dealers, all benefit from present cash-flow lending policies.

Quicksilver funds came into being because:

(1) Government promises zig and zag; often, radically altering the value of its currency. These promises create deficits that require additional money to keep coming in from revenue sources other than taxes (a damn poor substitute for a long-term economic policy).

(2) Big banks found a way of making huge profits without any risks by getting government to guarantee their loans, while changing from being banks to financial investment institutions.

(3) Big fees would be paid by those who needed

favors or money. And

(4) Institutional investors found financing deficits and speculating on new paper has a guaranteed return from rising interest rates that are the trademarks of inflated currencies.

For the average working family, banks have lost their purpose.

All the banks are going to do is — maybe — if you have a job, lend you money for a new car, a TV set, a boat, or some other non-income producing possession. And charge a fee for everything.

Why make asset-based loans when cash flow loans are guaranteed by the United States Government?

Why make small asset-based loans when those who have money, or access to money, will pay you large fees and commission for just taking care of their money? And maybe cut you in on the deal?

Why make little "piddly" asset-based sound and solid loans, when you can be a wheelin'-dealin' gambling high roller in a high-risk, high-stakes game of *cash*? (Especially, when you can set the value of the chips and change the rules of the game whenever you wish?)

Why not, when you keep your winnings and big fees, and when you lose, others are forced to cover your losses?

Why make asset-based loans when $500 billion in drug money is floating around, looking for a home?

Quicksilver funds are of relatively little benefit to millions of working men and women. They are not available to put food on our tables, clothes on our backs, or a roof over our heads. They are not available for us to use in acquiring hard assets, or for our use in creating an opportunity for our own economic improvement.

And, while forced by our government to guarantee a profit for a privileged few insiders, who own or manipulate these funds, we do not receive any of the profits because it goes to pay for management fees and a big bonus to top-management officers.

It is not in our best interest to have speculative swings in interest rates. A slumping dollar, any debasement of value, means working families must expend more energy just to stay even.

What happened to the 30-hour working week forecast in the late 60's? Now, often it takes two full-time working family members just to make ends meet.

A weak dollar, relative to other currencies, increases inflationary rates, and increases the prices we pay for goods and services.

Any benefits from quicksilver funds accruing to working families come with strings attached. Too many times, it is our access to money, and our money itself, going to pay for the bad judgment and the outright wrong doing of company officials, brokers and bank officers.

Quicksilver funds primarily are only of benefit to centralized governments, speculators, big banks and short-sighted conglomerates.

Quicksilver money does little to encourage confidence in our ability to compete, in enhancing confidence that we – and our children – have a chance at economic advancement, that economic opportunity still exists.

We have forgotten the basic purpose of banks, brokerage houses, mutual funds, pension funds, insurance companies, and of all the other institutional investors.

Banks came into being as the "go-between" those and who had it and those who could put it to work in endeavors likely to be successful. The "go-between" charged a fee for bringing them together and overseeing that the funds were used for the purpose they were intended...

This simple concept created opportunities for all

citizens to acquire hard assets to use in an economic endeavor of their choice. Activities by millions of citizens boosted long-term growth and a strong economy by creating new businesses and fostering the accumulation of new equipment, fixtures, inventory, while putting savings to work – and improving productivity.

Capital spending for project investment and new productivity is the traditional trademark of all sound economic development. These are the economic staples for the development of hard assets.

It is by creating opportunities for all citizens to acquire hard assets that countries, any country, can best assure sound and solid, long-term economic growth.

Volatility in financial markets, currency devaluation, or rising skepticism about the value of one's money, are not caused by creating assets, or asset based lending, or investment in assets. These are the trademarks of a government-bungling paper economy.

Quicksilver funds rely upon economic crises, market jitters and inflationary political gambits in their gamble for short-term profits.

In turn, speculative and dangerous economic policies are generated by the availability of quicksilver funds.

Economic instability is the result.

(Since 1988, the idea of Quicksilver, Hedge, Equity, Venture, bank, brokerage, whatever "fund" you want to call it – that requires a minimum of a million, fifty million or even a billion dollars to participate in the manipulation of the financial markets – have been repulsive. It is not an equal opportunity for small investors. And it damn sure is not providing the equal treatment under the law *demanded by the U. S. Constitution.)*

19 ECONOMIC SURVIVAL

Small businesses are an endangered species.

They face a horde of predators disguised as bankers, politicians, corporate executives and their quasi-domesticated herds of crooks, swindlers, mobsters, greedy takeover artists and power-seeking bureaucrats – and office buildings full of their lawyers!

If the role of government is to stop economic growth, it is now, with the active cooperation of the nation's bankers, the most efficient it has ever been.

With governmental approval, banks provide and administer the money supply.

They make loans to a few select borrowers and family friends. While President of an Eastern bank, John Bunting bragged, "We determine who will succeed and who will fail."

Small business owners, with viable, profitable, successful small businesses, were caught in a vicious quagmire by the fallout of bank failures in the mid-1980s; something the small business owners had no part in creating. Business and personal credit ratings were wounded or destroyed, performing loans were turned into bad loans by new bank lending policies, and owners were told to secure financing elsewhere (which was an almost impossible task with all lending practices the same at all banks).

It is most unusual for a new small business startup to do it with a loan from a bank today.

Small business loans are not available to any worthwhile degree from any source. But it is the small business owners and workers with little chance of economic advancement who are demanded to pay much of the bill presented by politicians.

The question is, "With what?"

Banks and large corporations are predators, feeding on ideas, inventions and efficiencies, the creativity of small businesses, whether the small business owner knows it or not.

In the late 1800's, when government was not a system for generalized welfare, the Sherman Act, among others, was enacted to establish a set of ground rules restricting monopolies. The Supreme Court ruled time and time again that monopolies were not in America's best interest. The court issued ruling after ruling that monopolistic business practices were not allowed.

Politicians must take the blame, along with the idiots who voted them into, and who keep them in office, for the growth of monopoly-minded predators, including the banking conglomerates of today.

There are about 50 licensed government bond dealers in the U. S., who can purchase government debt obligations directly from the U. S. Government.

Over $200 billion in government debt (government-backed securities) are open for interest-rate bids every week. Every week. But only 50 firms can place bids?

Isn't this an open door to financial wrong-doing?

Michael Milken, creator of Wall Street's biggest scandal, until 1995's experiment with the highly exotic derivatives, bilked billions of dollars from junk bonds and insider trading. Then, when finally convicted, Milken served only 22-months of a 10-year term at a minimum-security work camp, not a prison, but a so-called work camp near San Francisco.

Most of the convicted operators of failed thrifts never paid their assessed fines, nor have they served completed sentences of jail time.

Of the hundreds of crooks and fellow swindlers in some of the nation's largest brokerage houses and banks who guided Enron, WorldCom, and hundreds of other companies into ruin, only a handful ever saw jail time.

There must be a few scrapegoats and examples, you know...

Justice?

The average term for a car thief convicted in federal court is 28 months; but the average term for a convicted banker is 21 months. Under plea-bargains, over 100 crooked bankers, caught up in the financial shenanigans of the 1980s, fully escaped serving any prison time, and the promised restitution from these defendants amounts to only 0.043-percent: Less than a half penny on each dollar assessed.

According to the General Accounting Office, the investigatory arm of Congress, government officials recovered just 4.5-percent of the $846.7 million in fines and restitutions assessed in 2,603 criminal bank cases from October, 1988, through the end of 1992.

Even though most defendants did not pay up, the Justice Department touted the large fines and restitution orders as a sign of its success in prosecuting financial criminal cases.

Hey, Justice, *they kept the money!*

Some defendant's lawyers, government officials and defendants themselves admit that the fines "are unenforceable" and "do nothing more than give the appearance of government action."

Of $133,222,460 in fines on 109 bankers, under

plea bargain agreements, 99.57% is still outstanding, and likely will never be paid.

The $577,540 in fines paid for the savings and loan fiasco of the 1980s, was more than "wiped out" when the Resolution Trust Corporation paid $1,013,200 in bonuses to just 136 of the agency's top officials in 1992. *"We feel that these bonuses were justified,"* a *RTC spokesman claimed. "Other government agencies give bonuses."*

This is the kind of stuff that shows your tax dollars at work: Justice at its best – or worst.

And it doesn't end - ever: Donald Trump reached agreements with bankers who, in exchange for equity positions in projects of Trump Enterprises, forgave him of around $1 billion in personal debt. But when has your banker agreed to let you pay-off a debt for half the remaining principal - and forego interest?

Then, in the 2009-2100 bail-out of the nation's largest financial institutions, taxpayers rewarded the big banks – and the Trumps of the business world – by paying their bad loans.

Voters – taxpayers – have lost their economic mind:

Banks today speculate in the bond and securities markets; act as insurance agents, real estate agents and developers, equipment and auto leasing firms, venture capital firms, etc. Banks can and do own stock in grocery stores, tire dealerships, department stores, oil companies, utilities, building firms, credit card companies, and every other non-banking type businesses.

A bank should not own other kinds of businesses, nor stock in non-bank businesses: A bank creates money. People who have to get money by their own exertions ought not be put into competition against people who can create it and/or administer it.

Banks should be selling loans, not buying stocks and selling real estate, or leasing equipment and all the other things they are now doing. Neither should their subsidiary holdings.

For years, restrictions existed on banks entering "non-banking...such as the selling of securities and insurance," a 1990 quote by U.S. Senator Phil Gramm, a member of the Senate Banking Committee.

Oh?

In 1990 alone, NCNB Texas (then NationsBank and now Bank of America) and First City Bancorporation of Texas each formed new Houston-based banks to pursue stock purchases and/or sales, management buyouts, equity deals, re-capitalizations, expansion opportunities and divestitures for companies with market values ranging from ten million up.

In 1994, these "prohibited activities" became legal ways of doing business by banks. U.S. House and Senate Banking Committees, at the urging of the Federal Reserve Board, expanded their powers to engage in these and other_national and international activities.

Politicians, those kooks we kooks elect to office, gave banks the power to do these things!

And in the first months of 2016, our politicians have increased the national debt to around $19.2 trillion: $19,200,000,000,000.

If you gave someone a dollar every second it would take 32,000 years to give them $1 trillion, or over 608,000 years to give away $19 trillion.

Frito-Lay produces 1-billion potato chips each month. Want to figure out, at that rate, how many years it would take Frito-Lay to produce about 19-trillion chips?

Have fun . . .

If you want to see how high the numbers can go just add the $75 to $80 trillion we now owe in government credit programs that could go bankrupt.

This $75 to $80 trillion is rarely - if ever - mentioned in the government's annual budget. (Actually, there has not been an annual budget submitted to Congress in over seven years.) But these potential liabilities are in the form of loans, loan guarantees, insurance commitments and other credit programs.

Today, our debt is larger than our income.

The $325 to $500 billion tax-payer bail-out of banks in the late 80's came from just *one* government credit program. When there is no risk of failure, banks will always need more tax dollars.

In 1989, more than $3 billion in losses occurred in the co-insured and financed multi-family residential program in the Housing and Urban Development Department. All were government-guaranteed loans, backed by money to be collected from taxpayers, to make some crook rich, or some rich crook richer.

Then came 2008: Remember politicians weeping about "too big to fail'? The resulting bailout of the big financial institutions, and borrowers like General Motors, touch the $750 billion mark.

Our national budget has operated at a deficit for years on money borrowed from banks and foreign investors. We have spent years talking about the deficit while watching it growing faster than dandruff.

In 1995, the Republican controlled U. S. House passed a resolution giving the voters in each state a chance to vote on a balanced budget amendment to the Constitution. It failed. Six Democratic Senators, who had voted for such an amendment previously, voted with other Democratic Senators (and an Oregon Republican, Mark Hatfield) to refuse voters in the individual states a chance to approve or disapprove the amendment.

Politics are more important than our economic survival.

When Wright Patman was U.S. Representative from Texas' 1st Congressional District, he claimed in his book, PRIMER ON MONEY, *"Money is a manufactured item. The amount of money available to the economy is determined by the manufacturers - but under the Constitution, it is the right and duty of Congress to create money. It is left entirely to Congress. Congress has farmed out this power; has given it to the banking system."*

Patman was correct: Congress failed to carry out their responsibility by placing our economic lives in the hands of the Federal Reserve Bank, which is a system of private banks that control the money supply – and that, by law, guarantees the member banks a 6% annual profit.

If you, as many do, believe the "too big to fail" bailout was necessary because of a "slump in the oil and real estate markets, you have bought the fictional account that bankers and politicians want you to believe. Oil and real estate were only the vehicles to carry thousands of unwise, unethical and illegal transactions.

Jack T. Conn of the old Oklahoma City Fidelity Bank once said, "The largest single cause of bank failures is misuse of banking assets by directors and officers."

Karl Marx wrote: "...banking...and credit thus become...one of the most potent instruments of crises and swindles."

Financial institutions do not die of any natural economic cause. They are sucked dry by an army of swindlers, crooks, mobsters, and greedy (if not stupid) bankers, who, with the help of meddling, paid-for politicians and unethical lawyers, all engage in a host of insider deals.

It is those of us who pay local taxes, support local schools, churches, hospitals, chambers of commerce, etc.; who support little league baseball, boy and girl scouts, the United Way campaigns, etc.; who provide housing, services and goods, and who generate the greatest number of jobs; who are forced to pay for the centralization and collectivism of the American economy.

Government forces the small business people (Mom and Pop, most of us) to pay the bills, but deny us the means to secure the tools (capital) which we can use to develop viable new small businesses and community and economic projects to get ahead economically ourselves.

According to studies by the SBA, MIT, and numerous others, small businesses account for three out of every five jobs. In many rural states, some estimates report that 90% of the jobs are created by small businesses.

Over the last thirty years, Americans have seen our better-paying jobs shipped out of the country. And some large corporations downsized jobs to part-time to avoid insurance, retirement and other job-related benefits. During the same time, choice in goods and services dwindled down to a few big box stores selling the same things in the same kinds of stores; only the labels are different.

As long as funds for small businesses continue to remain unavailable, the economy not only will be a downhill roller coaster ride, but job-creation will continue to decline, family incomes fall, and new domestic investment will continue to stagnate, especially, as the crooks, bankers and politicians (and their friends) continue to feather their nests while promising *tomorrow* to taxpayers.

Politicians, non-profit enterprise development groups, bankers, etc., continue a steady stream of press releases, conferences, studies, hearings, etc., on economic and policy measures and reports.

Most of these endeavors criticize the nation's economy as it continues to show signs of instability and spotty recovery; and point hopefully to ways for government to support and underwrite large multi-nationals' entries into areas of "world trade in a world economy."

When it comes to doing something positive about the weaknesses displayed in our national economy, these groups not only are passive but generally, are calling for more of what created the weaknesses.

You do not ask weasels how to build chicken coops.

Not one candidate for a statewide or national office in recent years has called for a mandated policy requiring a percentage of all local deposits be made to small business asset-based loans by the financial institutions in communities where the deposits originate.

Not one candidate has said, "Assets are valuable."

We have an economy that will continue to have wide swings in stability, and areas of weakness, as long as we continue to ignore the economic foundation for our economy.

We must have an even playing field for economic opportunities.

Today's economic and banking policies create growing disparities between rich and poor, between rural and urban areas, and between the artificial paper profits for a few and real economic prosperity for our nation.

What metropolitan center bank has a commercial or even a development loan program for under $3 million? How many will even make a loan based on assets or even the net equity in assets?

How many (of the total number) families, individuals, or businesses need, or can even afford, a $1 million loan?

But the same banks that will not make the small business or investment loan are delighted to have the small deposits, the smaller savings and checking accounts: They will be very glad to take them and lend them to the large players in international markets and here at home.

Taxpayers are forced to guarantee the few financial institutions a profit, but those same institutions will not make an asset-based loan.

Does this seem equal?

Where is economic justice when our lending institutions declare our assets are worthless? And who gives them the right to do so? Where is economic justice when our assets are not worth a loan from a bank?

Walter E. Williams who taught economics at George Mason University in Fairfax, Virginia, once observed: "Economic justice at least includes a set of circumstances whereby I keep my earnings and you keep yours; government does not take your money and give it to me, nor does it take mine to give to you."

A question we ask, that only you can answer, is, "What percentage of your earnings belongs to somebody else?"

Economic justice is certainly not a corporate welfare system.

Economic opportunity does not exist in a closed economic system operated under job conditions rated almost next to slavery.

Today, *opportunity* is just a word.

In a year when Corning Glass Works received *a $1.5 million grant* from the Department of Housing and Urban Development, Corning's sales were nearly $2 billion.

Another $15 million of our earnings were given by HUD to the City of Detroit to prepare a plant site for Chrysler Corporation. Chrysler's earnings that year were $21.2 billion. Welfare for the corporate rich and those who have money should make you sick.

If it doesn't, it should at least make you angry: it is *your* economic survival that's on the line...

And it is our nation's future on the line.

Where is the economic justice when the large banks use deposits and savings of families of moderate means and the surviving small businesses to speculate on foreign currencies and to make large loans to large corporations?

Where is the economic justice when government guidelines encourage such practices, but discourage small loans for asset formulation by individuals?

The corporate welfare system finds the large banks at the front of the "free lunch" line, and with both feet in the trough: They use a host of government-backed loans to claim they are serving small businesses. These are loans for low-income housing to $1,000,000 homes for the rich, for education for all, for minority enterprise investment companies that are subsidiaries of the rich and powerful, and for Small Business Administration guaranteed loans –

These are not bank loans, but government welfare programs for the large banks, administered by the banks, and presented as "small business" bank loans.

It's almost laughable.

Even a small business under SBA guidelines can net $1.7 million annually and have assets of up to $3,000,000 and sales of up to $10,000,000 annually. These are not "small" businesses.

Today, big government, conglomerates and big banks form an almost unbreakable barrier to small, private economic opportunities. While they may squabble among themselves over what economic pie will be sliced next, who controls the slicing, and who gets what slice; they are the ones who get the pie.

Individuals and small businesses, that created and baked it, are allowed the few crumbs that may fall to the floor.

R. Crosby Kemper, while Chairman of United Missouri Bancshares, Inc., which owned several area Missouri banks, blamed real estate lending for the nation's economic ills of the 80's: "...caused by stupid real estate lending to finance un-needed projects, first by savings and loans and now by our brethren in the banking industry."

Mr. Kemper is a banker. What he did not say is that too many large loans to a few large corporations created a glut in large metropolitan areas. Kemper also did not confess that too many large loans to a few large corporations created no new jobs, or few new investments in plants or equipment.

Kemper, and his other brother bankers, would prefer that large loans to large corporations for mergers, buyouts and takeovers (that fail and cost billions), be their "preferred customer".

While acknowledging that not all large loans are bad, and must be available in the marketplace, it must be understood that making ONLY large loans is a bad and unwise policy.

Making only large cash-flow loans guarantees economic stagnation over the long haul.

Money must be available to small businesses for a variety of income-producing projects and endeavors.

Opportunities for job-creation, for creating savings in assets, for developing pride in ourselves and in our communities, and for patching cracks in our economic foundations, must exist and be available to build a strong economy.

If capital were available to small businesses, it could also have the related effect of reducing the number of huge multi-million and multi-billion dollar loans, the resulting losses from some such loans, and the increases in reserves needed for those loans (which also depletes needed capital available for new projects).

The realization, of course, is that no one has all the answers. But, if one can understand a problem, one should be able to make some recommendations for solution.

Some recommendations may be impossible to do, because of a variety of *"not politically-feasible"* reasons (as some will claim). But some corrections in our economic system, to enhance flexibility in desirable economic opportunities, as touched on in earlier chapters, must be fully explored.

One correction needed is a requirement, enforced with discretion, in terms of averages rather than minimums, that term loans and mortgages in banks match up with totals of savings accounts and time deposits other than CDs.

A requirement that a percentage (say, 40%), of a bank's deposits is made in loans within the local community (many of the branches in local communities are now nothing more than conduits for local deposits to banks headquartered in a Metropolitan center).

A requirement that a percentage of a bank's deposits be made in loans that are based on assets, rather than cash flows. This, alone, would act to increase national savings rates (as investments are a form of savings).

Small business owners generally have assets and are in markets that support a relatively small cash flow, but that add immeasurable to national productivity and GNP when combined together. And investments in assets create cash-flow streams.

Access to development capital is a must.

There should be a requirement that a percentage of the loans of any bank be set for small asset-based term loans of $500,000 and under. This would provide badly needed capital for small businesses.

Loans of over $100 million, or some such number, should be required to go through SEC registration, like long-term debt instruments. This would also allow more opportunities for investment by small investors.

In light of the consolidation of Exxon-Mobil and the other big oil companies, the merger of big drug, big agriculture, and other firms, the debacles at Enron, Intergrated Resources, WorldCom, Drexel-Burnham-Lambert, Lehman Brothers, Goldman-Sachs, and the hundreds of others, any enforcement of antitrust laws is now a farce (whatever the Justice Department or the courts may say or do.)

Shouldn't public transparency be required on all institutions using deposits, shares, fees, etc.?

There should be a requirement that a lending institution publish at the end of each quarter disclosure of all new loans made in that quarter by categories more detailed than now reported. (Get the truth out: How much in loans to conglomerates; how much to retailers and manufacturers; how much to public utilities; how much in residential and commercial mortgages? And what is the ratio of all loans to deposits, by category, within a defined local area and the amount outside the local area.)

At least, a public disclosure of the percentage of a bank's deposits that are invested in government-debt?

And shouldn't disclosure of assets be included? How much invested in stocks of non-bank businesses, including bank-owned real estate holdings or bank or other development companies, government securities, related financial lending firms, etc.

There should be a requirement restricting non-bank activities and non-bank business ownership by banks. Businesses looking for capital should never be forced to compete with those owned by the businesses with the power to create the capital.

And, most importantly, banks should be required to write term loans at a fixed interest rate: No variable rate mortgages which, in effect, convert long-term assets into short-term assets.

Because of the Variable Interest Rate, long term loans have basically been eliminated. What were term loans are now only 6-month to 7-year loans, with a "promise" of rollover when due.

Under current practices, a Variable Interest Rate loan is not a long-term loan. When a variable rate loan is used for long-term production needs, the loan is automatically un-payable when due (and when a "promise" of rollover is not met by the financial institution, some insider is likely the new owner with a new loan.

The risks of interest rate fluctuations, the rise or fall of interest rates, should be borne by the banks, which supposedly are the professionals in money markets, and not by their customers. (Why should a bank's customer socialize the bad judgment of a banker, which the variable interest rate more or less does..?)

Eliminating the variable interest rate would also, in effect, discourage rapid rate movements in money-markets, and at the same time delay and discourage inflationary pressures in the money-markets.

While many of these recommendations are desirable and needed, none of these changes will come about as long as the bankers and large corporations continue to be the major dynamic force in American politics.

Politicians will let this status quo continue until a majority of the voters make their opinions known. Politicians react; they do not lead.

Self-entitlement, not self-enlightenment, is the forte of crooks, bankers, and all stripes of politicians.

Numerous species have disappeared from this world because of this same short-sighted view of their worlds.

And it is a view that is causing our nation to become just another third world economy.

Our private enterprise system has disappeared.

Asset acquisition and development by individuals and small businesses create the jobs, provide the power that begins turning the economic wheel, and generates local investments. But as long as paper can show an artificial profit, the creators of paper-profits will continue to "kill the goose that laid the golden egg."

If economic opportunities are to remain the base of

sound economic growth, under a system of economic freedom, voters must act to protect small businesses – and themselves – if they are to remain anything more than an endangered species.

Politicians and community activists continually talk about "the need for diversification of the economic base." It sounds wise, and everyone wants to progress up the living scale, but the words are not the reality. It is the call for more government.

Widening of the economic base, generating new economic activity, is impossible without some sources for capital for land, building, equipment, inventories, etc. All of which are the assets which, in turn, generate cash flows.

These things are also investments and savings.

A community that wants to "diversify its economic base" first must have a source that lends money on assets.

Why politicians, economists, and community and economic development experts fail to understand that local economies can only deteriorate under a policy of cash-flow loans can only be left for bureaucrats and lawyers to explain by lying to themselves.

It is evident that, so far, very little they have done over the last 50-years relates to common sense.

Bankers, bureaucrats, and politicians, surprisingly, do not understand money; they only understand theories of money.

When it comes to money, the bankers, with the variable interest rates of today, raise the rate of interest; bureaucrats know that their departments are entitled to shear the sheep every year or so; and the good ol' boy politicians simply have a fund-raising campaign, or invite a group of lobbyists to breakfast.

Those who do not understand money think money is easy to come by, especially if you don't have to do something productive for it . . .

Lawyers and stockbrokers, and their related kith

and kin, also do not understand theories of money: Lawyers sue somebody, and stock brokers either buy/sell/manipulate another issue of some stock, or some new derivative of such, using someone else's money and taking their cut from it.

Our economy today has a few large investors, either brokerages, banks, fund managers, etc., who don't produce anything; and another 5,000-or so large conglomerates with money managers who simply engage in acquisitions, mergers, or buyouts.

Very few of these really make any new things.

We have, with Congressional approval, an economy that moves tons and tons of paper. As this trend has taken root, allowed by misallocation of capital resources, we have produced fewer and fewer things.

And our politicians and their fee-paid fuzz-brained economists cannot seem to understand why our citizens show voter anger, and disgust with the system in general.

When you produce less, your national wealth will decline.

A second thing that happens when you produce less is that you must go overseas to buy more of what you want because you are not making it at home.

The third thing is the debt-service on all your huge loans soon eats up your profits.

Next, the ole boys overseas – who sold you all those things you stopped producing – buy your bankrupt business for 10-or less cents on the dollar.

And he does it with your dollars.

Then comes the final blow: Bankers run to the shark, who just took over your business, and make him a huge unsecured (just on his cash flow) loan to buy more businesses.

...and the whole cycle starts all over again, but with fewer wheels. And the bigger wheels just keep grinding up the smaller wheels and the wobbles become more obvious.

Watching all this, more and more people give up hope.

How can we, as the nation that created economic hope, and created the world's greatest economy, fail to recognize the fundamental foundation of how we got to be the most powerful nation in history?

Why do we continue to elect political leaders who restrict and destroy the creative energies of the individual?

Do we not realize that the politician knows it is much, much easier to control a few thousand corporate entities than millions of individuals?

Is it simply a matter of control by the progressive/regressives in charge; is it the exercise of power, just for the exercise of power? Or is it greed? Or is it just a matter of plain stupidity?

It can't be ignorance; they know better.

If we know better and we continue to let matters remain unchallenged, if we do not require some changes in the way we do the proper business of government, our children will get exactly what we deserve.

Our politicians and bankers no longer talk in dollar terms of a million or so.

Nowadays, the numbers are in the billions and trillions. And we let them. The numbers are so high they're over our heads. And we should say, *"Whoa! Stop this nonsense!"*

We should demand some reality.

The Zippo Manufacturing Company, of Bradford, Pennsylvania, about 130-miles northeast of Pittsburg, cranked out its 400-millionth lighter on September 3, 2003. Four Hundred Million are a lot of lighters. But they have been cranking them out since 1932, or for about 83/84-years.

But to our politicians and our bankers, 400-million anymore is nothing significant.

The term they use for $400 million is "just chump

change."

Well, we're the chumps.

For there is no change.

The American voter is the chump because we allowed them to make us chumps.

We are the chumps because we won't demand the necessary changes.

We're allowing the socialist to eat our lunch.

20 A FAIR SHARE...?

"Fair Share" is a Marxist concept because the Elite leadership will determine the relative definition of "Fair Share" and who gets what and how much.

When it comes to a "Fair Share", the Marxist Elite and their political cronies will get the major share, just as they did in Russia, Cuba, Argentina, China, Venezuela, North Korea, et al.

Unfortunately, the nation's progressives (socialists) controlled or influenced by such Marxist promoters have made "Fair Share" the war cry in their loud and continuous efforts to weaken and destroy our American Constitution.

This demand of a "Fair Share" is a term that can have multiple meanings. First, the intent is to replace our Constitutional right to "equal protection under the law" with "fair share" – a term that can have multiple meanings.

The sudden switching to a "fair share" argument is dangerous to American concepts of private property rights and of our liberty.

As used by the modern socialists, the term "fair share" is a term of word art; usually as a part of a larger discussion about the correlative rights of private individuals and private property. "Word masters" without principles use "fair share" to hide or direct attention away from our Constitutional right to "equal protection under the law".

And this sudden switch to a "fair share" argument is dangerous to our liberty:

Centuries of constitutional, case and legislative law development prove that our wise and moral Founders showed us that the most effective core principle for combating any institutionalized discrimination by government (including rogue communal planning committees, state-controlled regional politburos, special interest, etc.,) against private ownership is "equal protection under the law".

Not "fair share".

We each own our own life, and no one or no government body has a "Fair Share" right to it.

Under the encroaching socialist manipulation of the term "Fair Share", even our courts, including the Supreme Court in a few cases, have resorted to "fair share" in dicta (words not used in the ruling of the case) under some erroneous assumption that there was a concept of scarcity in the case before them.

They forgot or ignored the fact that the term "Fair Share" is not found in the Constitution.

But it is more commonly associated with and permeates Marx' thinking as seen in Chapter Two of the Communist Manifesto.

The Marx' Hegelian-derived attitude of scarcity brutally denies private property ownership rights for the false "greater" communist good.

It is in the concept of individual human worth that our nation's founders first developed the mandates for a form of government limited in its power and as the servant of the people – not their master – and set them in a Constitutional construct.

Consider that for over two hundred years, when we buy land, we buy more than just dirt. Our home is our castle. We buy an estate in land that includes the right to prevent trespass against the whole world including those lawless administrative state agents who would force us to curtail the use of our private property into perpetuity for state-enforced environmental and investment purposes (think Soviet economics); and work as servants of the government (think communist communes).

These are governmental actions, clearly an unlawful Taking for which they do not offer to pay us, thereby enslaving us in our own homes and on our own land. Government takes control of our private property by forcing us to use it in ways that we don't want to. The Fourth Amendment clearly states that the federal government cannot force us to work for it. And there is no statute of limitations for slavery – as prohibited by the 13th Amendment.

It's called private property because it is privately managed.

Marx called landowners the "bourgeoisie". Stalin called the landed peasants of Ukraine "kulaks". Hitler called Jews "vermin". Occupy Wall Street vilified "the wealthy 1%"(as did the Bernster and Honest Hillary). Argentina calls elderly pensioners who want all their pension money "vultures".

And in 2015, Texas State Representative James L. "Jim" Keffer (R-District 60), called private groundwater owners "hoarders", a term generally referring to a mental disorder.

Too many candidates for public office promise they will work for "fair play" and for a "fair share".

But it is "Equal protection under the law" that prevents monopolies and giant conglomerates rigging of the system, and discrimination by those serving in government.

"Equal protection" is available only to humans. Not fish, not down-stream flows and not the environmental commune.

But the same cannot be said of "fair share'. How large is the "fair share" of our Rights and private property that we must give up?

Under "equal protection under the law", you own 100% of your property and have certain rights guaranteed by the Constitution, and the administrative state owns 100% of its property and has certain rights under the Constitution.

If government wants to devilishly force you to curtail your use of your property, then it must pay you *Just Compensation* as required by law.

The administrative state can do whatever it wants with its own property.

But when we allow the government in its legislative or administrative function to take away part of our individual rights, there is nothing that they can "pay" us for it.

The socialistic top-down centralized planners and controllers (believing in Marx' "socio-economics") must pay you for the property they take from you. But any taking our rights through the implied threat of violence (massive daily fines) is an alteration of the U. S. Constitution.

If a politician strays too far to the right, if he or she appears to promote an idea that is outside the collective, one that seemingly advocates personal freedom based on personal responsibility, then they are going to be hammered by a national news media filled with our nation's socialist Hegelian and Keynesian sycophants. They will be hammered by the know-nothing talking air-heads in the television industry; hammered by the their left-leaning peers in the House and Senate; and personally attacked by the paid flunkies serving their socialist-leaning masters in both major political parties.

And there will be an all-out effort by those on the left to hammer them at the ballot box or run them out of town for being a "conservative extremist".

But if one of the socialist members of the nationwide collective, criminally destroys important papers that are national records, or treasonably gives aid and comfort to our nation's enemies by an illegal administrative edict, they are enthusiastically and wildly applauded by the dangerous dummies who are the believers in and the dupes of the national collective.

There are always those who have a masochistic willingness to destroy themselves and the country that gives them the freedom to voice the nuttiest ideas.

Often, the nuttier the better: Remember, *Hope and Change* and *Make America Great Again?*

There is no excuse for national stupidity.

21 THE FEDERAL RESERVE SYSTEM

We are, supposedly, a free society with common agreements on rules and standards of civil behavior, based on a free market with common agreements on rules and standards for economic opportunity for each individual.

Well, our free market ain't so, joe.

Thirteen individuals control the money supply and the entire monetary health of the United States. These thirteen individuals are private bankers, or individuals recommended by bankers, who control vast sums of money.

This is the way the Federal Reserve System was planned and organized and developed by J. P. Morgan and a few of his banking associates in 1913, and later approved by the U.S. Congress.

The Federal Reserve System is not a public institution, and it is not a national central bank, but it is supposed to act as one. But, in fact, it is a private institution, controlled by the larger banks, for the primary benefit of large banks, and is probably the most profitable enterprise in America.

None of the Federal Reserve Banks are government institutions: They are owned by private banking institutions who hold the stock of the Federal Reserve Banks (that control all the money); and the governing boards and officers of these banks are selected by private bankers. There is no monitoring or oversight by any unit or office of government.

It is a profit-making entity, entirely independent of the budgetary process.

The actual work of the Federal Reserve Board is carried out by the nation's largest private banks.

At the national level, each of the thirteen individuals who make-up the Federal Reserve Board are appointed by the President to six-year terms. Since the terms of the members are staggered, a president serving two full four year terms in office is likely, however, to be able to appoint only two Board members.

These appointments usually are upon the recommendations of bankers who have made the most contributions to the president's campaign for office.

These thirteen individuals appoint all the other members of the Reserve District banks, and none of the appointees are subject to confirmation by the U. S. Congress.

While District Reserve banks may have "Advisory Directors" who are not bankers, and these "Advisory Directors" may recommend policies, they do not have voting privileges on policy matters.

All Federal Reserve Board meetings are in secret. Not even the President of the United States can attend Board meetings.

For the last fifty years, House and Senate Banking Committees act merely to "rubber stamp" actions, policies, regulations and recommendations made by the Fed.

The United States Constitution gives the power and the authority for the control of the nation's money to Congress. Congress has farmed this power out to the nation's bankers.

A quick look at the history of the System raises doubts about its role in the American economy. One of their first acts was to outlaw the exchange of gold as a currency by American citizens. Next, their efforts resulted in the issuance of "silver certificates" for currency purposes. Then, when they failed to grab enough of these certificates in their greedy hands, the Feds did away with them.

Next, the American dollar was "pegged" at $35 for one ounce of gold. Then, in 1973, the big bankers mugged the dollar again when they succeeded in having President Nixon remove the dollar from the gold standard and "let the dollar float."

Next, came inflation – followed by price and wage controls and runaway inflation at the highest rate in peacetime history.

Before you could blink, in economic time, it took four hundred dollars to buy that same ounce of gold. (Author's note: Now, in 2016, it takes about $1,400 to buy that same ounce of gold. But the government's economic experts tell us that inflation is under control...)

It was not that gold was more valuable, or there was any less of it: Overnight, our dollars lost a great deal of their value. This was simply because dollars were based on "good faith" and not on an asset. The value of the dollar now was being set by the big banks.

The dollar is only as valuable as the bankers say it is... Paper money is only as valuable as the nation's belief in a trustworthy government.

If you could set the value of the chips in a poker game, and could change the value of each chip when you wanted to, how could you lose...?

If you were in a game where another player had the right to change the rules of the game when he wanted to, along with the value of each score, how often do you think you would win?

And wouldn't you be an idiot to sit in any game where another player had those powers? Well, you are...as our economy is a game where other players have just such powers.

Why did the Federal Reserve Board, the big bankers, want the change? What good would it do them? Because the big banks had billions and billions of dollars out on loan at extremely high interest rates to a lot of foreign countries.

These Third World, and mostly South American, countries were not able to pay the interest, let alone the principal, on these billion dollar loans.

By weakening the dollar, creating immediate inflation that caused immediate dollar devaluation, the large banks had a chance of eventually being paid some of the interest owed and, hopefully, some of the principal.

The value of our dollar wasn't as important as their profit (even on paper).

Don't believe it? Here, in their words, is what they believe: *("The committee judges that, on balance, the risk of inflation becoming undesirably low is likely to be the predominant concern for the foreseeable future."* Statement from the Federal Reserve Board's Open Market Committee report, August, 2003.)

According to most scholars, the Great Depression concentrated enormous amounts of wealth into a few hands. For every one thousand-or-so losers, there was one big winner who was a banker, or a friend of a banker.

In the early 90's, the same old scene was playing to a slightly different tune.

Between 1990 and 1995, over a 5-year period, millions of small investors lost billions of dollars.

But as the economy went in the tank, a few big companies started merging with a fewer bigger companies (with the government's permission), and most of the financial crooks escaped jail, or even a requirement of payback.

Banks largely determine who will succeed and who will fail. They do so by the lending policies and practices as set by the Federal Reserve Board. The Feds change the rules of the game of lending and borrowing, and set the value of the dollar...when they want to...as they want to...because they control the supply of money.

It is these regulations along with policies to allow for, and/or to curb, inflation that determine the health of the American economy.

Our economy is at the mercy of – controlled by – the Federal Reserve Board.

Actions of the Feds have the blessing of 535-elected politicians.

ALL actions of the Fed are to guarantee a profit to their members, all private bankers, regardless of how such actions may affect the economic fortunes of average citizens.

These bankers have friends, a small number of commercial and quasi-commercial conglomerates that are draining our nation's resources, destroying our assets, and forcing most Americans into a form of economic slavery.

These monopolies and conglomerates are doing these things with the active blessings, encouragement and approval of the Federal Reserve System.   But there is a vast societal cost, vast expenditures, in maintaining big banks and large conglomerates. The more they cost, the more of our resources they demand. The more necessary they can convince us they are, the more powerful they become.

The quasi-commercial enterprises are those depending upon funds, collected from taxpayers and given as grants and low-cost loans, from myriad government offices.   They demand money for the stated purpose of developing high-tech research centers and research facilities. They demand money to "keep us competitive" and to "maintain our leadership position in a free world."

Our conglomerates want us to believe that not only do we need them, we need them in order to succeed. They funnel funds to politicians who, in turn, funnel even more of our tax dollars to the conglomerates. This perpetuation of each other is in and of itself, an economic tyranny.

It also promotes the perception that these few, special, privileged monopolies are the protectors of us: their victims.

The Fed, the big banks, and their friends, the conglomerates, are killing economic opportunity. And our political leaders wonder why our economy is so unstable, why so many peaks and valleys...

Someone, sometime, somewhere, once observed that all organizations eventually turn into some form of government. They develop their own infrastructures, policies, programs, look for members of a like kind and develop group, or organizational, goals. They, either deliberately or not, shut out or discourage from membership those individuals who do not share the organization's reasons for existence. As an active organization of a like-minded group, its basic purpose eventually becomes the survival of the organization.

The basic goals of most organizations are to resist restrictions placed against them; to expand their growth; and add to their influence.

In short, the nature of government is to resist restrictions and to seek unfettered expansion and expression of itself. It does not matter whether the "form" of government is a private corporation, a social club, a democracy, a dictatorship or a few big bankers who make up the Federal Reserve System.

It is the nature of power.

The Federal Reserve System is a government by itself: a government within the government.

The Federal Reserve Board controls the economy. They, along with a few wealthy elite individuals and monopolies hold most of the dollars and control, one way or another, most of the assets.

Money will always find a way to get what it wants.

The Federal Reserve System, the Federal Reserve Board, the big banks, the Federal Deposit Insurance Corporation, the Office of the Comptroller, all of the frame-work that makes up the System, have lost sight of what is good for America.

It is an uncontrolled, non-governed, unrestricted, private army of money-handlers, who are a government unto themselves, engaged in a war to control wealth creation by maintaining control of the money supply.

Congressman Patman, as previously noted, said that Congress has farmed out its authority and responsibility to the Feds. And, there is no functioning group trying to impose restrictions on it. The system has become an economic tyranny, forcing too many of our citizens into economic slavery.

For those who know how, or have the power, to manipulate currency, the Federal Reserve Board is a sound political decision (to gain their goals), but the Board's policy is an irresponsible fiscal policy, as it forces economic hardships on those who are the least empowered to express their rights.

Policies and regulations of the Federal Reserve Board are concerned primarily with retaining power, using disparity between those who have some and those who have little as a means of gaining control over everything.

They do so with the blessings of our elected officials: There are those in government who find excuses in this inequitable situation for imposing national social objectives that increase their own areas of power.

The big bankers who make up the Federal Reserve System are mortal men, not godlike creatures of infinite wisdom, nor are they heroes.

They are as imperfect as any group of citizens: You can always find at least one bad apple in a barrel full of apples.

The System presently has unchecked power, and it does not share power.

The only segment of American society where there is not some check on total power is the Federal Reserve System. They set policies, recommendations, rules and regulations without the consent of those forced to conform to them, and which restrict the economic choice of most individual citizens.

As the Fed goes its merry way, the General Accounting Office, in a 1995 report, showed that the System's operating costs rose at twice the rate of inflation between 1988 and 1994.

Auditors said they found a system-wide shortage of spending controls at the Fed.

In 1994, the Fed earned revenue of $24 billion and incurred expenses of $3.1 billion. The System contributed $20.5 billion of profit to the U. S. Treasury, after keeping $3.7 billion in a reserve fund. The Fed collects fees from the nation's commercial banks for providing such services as check clearing, and earns interest on government securities held by the System.

And they are guaranteed a 6% profit by law.

Oh, well: The Fed, at least, pays its own way, which is more proof that it is not a government agency.

And it seems we need and must have a central banking system. But what we have acts and behaves as any other government agency; as a fast-growing bureaucracy.

But, a few checks and balances, some oversight and accountability, must be reinstated into our nation's economic system.

Restrictions – not regulations – are needed.

Not all of our enemies are outside America.

We have done a wonderful job of growing our own...

22 ECONOMIC FORECASTERS

There are a lot of experts, mostly self-described, in the business of forecasting business cycles and economic trends.

Every day, dozens of television channels show some economic genius spouting off about esoteric theories and explaining phenomenon that we more simple mortals simply can't understand; especially, if they are market-makers who are buying and selling stocks.

Without these self-described experts, how would we know when to buy steak or beans?

Even if they knew how, without their government subsidizes, most of our economic experts would be lucky to have a bean to put in a pot.

Expert economists are curious creatures and, remarkably, some people view them as sane for the prominence their positions are given. This is also very curious...as it causes other people to wonder about the sanity of the viewer, as there is little doubt about that of the expert economist.

As the American economy continues to slide down to the toilet, there are more and more economists appearing on television screens. It seems that bad times bring out more economists

Once bad times begin, more bad things just seem to happen. And the more economic experts there are, the more confusion there is; especially, about why they are needed.

Like marketing experts, most are just good for using up good air.

But these economic forecasters tell us things that would make a dollar blush.

Today, the technology and those good ol' hedge funds tend to manipulate most things in such a blur that we don't know what we're doing or even where we're going. In a matter of a few seconds, businesses worldwide can be either good, bad or indifferent.

And some people who are friends with government can make billions of dollars disappear and no one knows where they go.

So now, we have magicians appearing, along with more economists.

These economic forecasters tell us that if there is a war, the economy might boom or the economy will collapse as trade is cut off.

And what usually happens in response to such claims is that Exxon raises its retail gas prices.

Sometimes, as we all know, something drastic does happen. The government will need a lot of money very quickly (which happens to most of us, and to all governments, frequently).

Our government, every year since 1972, has speeded up the printing presses just a little more each year and, today, most citizens don't have any money.

So, is there really any wonder about why our money doesn't have the purchasing power it once did?

The fact that inflation keeps nibbling away our money's value is fairly good proof that it is not worth much anymore.

But the money of other governments are also worth less.

This is not good, despite what the economists keep telling us – while bragging on the stock market.

These nincompoops tell us that when government takes money from one pocket and puts it into another it "creates economic activity".

They swear that it does, and they are the experts. At least, they are experts in causing other people to do a lot of swearing.

Weaving plausible sounding incomprehensible phases and talking about such technical analysis tools as RSI, MACD, Stochastics, Elliott Waves, Bollinger Bands et al., these economic forecasters smile at us from the television screens and predict a change from positive to negative and vice versa.

The cause of all this, they tell us, is very simple and obvious to them. But all we know is that our money is gone and someone else has it, and we will never see it again.

These economic geniuses claim that the cause of uncertainty in the markets is obvious, as it comes from outside our economic system, and is imposed by some uncertain source.

This is always good news, for *what would we do* if the uncertainty was inside the system, and the disturbing force was our government?

But that could not happen, because our lucid, observant, well-educated, full of wisdom populace keeps all politicians accountable.

And everyone knows it is not an advantage for politicians to keep people dumbed down, phlegmatic, distracted by celebrities and the latest new phone or app – and dependent on government programs.

Surely, the disturbing force couldn't be a system the politicians have established so they can keep winning election after election?

If money growth were necessary for economic growth, the last 30-or so years would have been a great time. During this period, the Federal Reserve tripled the total money supply, but the real economy - the buying power of the dollar - lost value, inflation grew by over 30 percent, and more families faced more economic hardships.

So, something is very wrong.

Today, money is printed primarily for the benefit of the politicians, the financial institutions and the special interests they serve. The value of our money is only what the government says it is.

So, obviously, its' only value is our faith in government. And our politicians tell us, re-assure us, that our expanding national economy "requires an ever-growing supply of money and credit in order to assure economic stability."

Of course it does (pardon our sarcasm): For hasn't the last forty years of almost continuous monetary expansion given us more economic stability?

Or a time mostly characterized by unprecedented economic instability?

Decades upon decades of inflation made Wall Street richer – and average Americans poorer.

It is our fault for listening to the mystical mutterings of political hacks and know-nothing underlings serving some special interest, and our government playing favorites and creating special privileges for them.

Under today's State Capitalism, big businesses enjoying their partnership with big government want us to believe that we must have "free market capitalism" in America.

Those of us who don't know any better, believe the lie and agree.

But State Capitalism is socialism, not capitalism. It is a welfare program for big business.

In a system of *real* free-market capitalism, there are *numerous producers* of a variety of innumerable goods and services, large and small, and most of them seldom ever get together, even for happy hour.

Under this new name for socialism, those joining together, especially in Washington, D. C. merriment, are engaging in non-business practices that can sometimes be highly profitable to the few. These insiders - those in political favor - drive out the good businesses and the good business practices by placing honest businesses at a competitive disadvantage. They do this while screaming loudly and often about "free market capitalism", but *not equal treatment under the law.*

And this is how we got into, ended up in, State Capitalism, but there is nothing "free" about it - except for a few government-approved conglomerates that are "free" to gouge private consumers.

We got here because the costs going into those "campaign" chests and political action committees (PACs) can be high.

BUT if no competition is so good, how is it that countries with centralized governments and a few state-approved businesses, engaging in no competitive actions, have such *low-quality products?*

Or do the low-quality products come from a few big businesses that just don't care, because there is no competition to fear?

A few of us do remember when the United States had a Private Enterprise System.

It wasn't that long ago when our economic system had a few strong restrictions against monopolies and predatory business practices, and banks encouraged small business startups with asset-based loans (none of today's only cash-flow loans for big businesses). And we had the world's best reputation for producing the *most* goods and the *most* variety of *quality* products.

But we allowed our politicians exchange the world's best economic system for *cronyism*.

It is up to the generations of today to challenge the status quo; to rise up and, as Jason did with the Golden Fleece, bring it back.

When it comes to government and business, small is better.

About the author

Jake Street is an interpreter of issues and values pertaining, but not limited, to politics, government, and economics as they emerge in American history and culture.

He is the author of two previous books, *The Texas Water War* and *Political Fiddlefaddle*, plus numerous magazine and website articles.

Currently, he is at work on a new book regarding popular culture, economy shenanigans and the destruction of every citizens' Constitutional guarantee of *equal treatment under the law.*